Pacific People and Their Food

Edited by

A B Blakeney
BRI Australia Ltd
Sydney, Australia

L O'Brien
University of Sydney
Narrabri, Australia

American Association of Cereal Chemists
St. Paul, Minnesota, USA

Library of Congress Catalogue Number: 98-86564
International Standard Book Number: 1-891127-03-9

Printed in Australia

American Association of Cereal Chemists
3340 Pilot Knob Road
St. Paul, Minnesota 55121-2097, USA

Preface

The Pacific Rim Symposia series was commenced by the AACC in 1993 with the first meeting being convened in Honolulu Hawaii.

Established to promote scientific interchange among the Associations growing international membership, the series has since seen successful symposia convened in Japan, Hong Kong and Singapore.

The decision to hold the Fifth Pacific Rim Symposium in Cairns, Australia in conjunction with the 48 th Australian Cereal Chemistry Conference of the Royal Australian Chemical Institute, Cereal Chemistry Division provides all cereal scientists from Australia, North America and the Pacific Rim region with the opportunity to meet at an international forum. Convened by the AACC, the Association hosts these symposia as part of its commitment to servicing its membership, especially those that reside outside of north America.

The theme for the Fifth Symposium, "Pacific People and their Food" was developed because of the recognition that the Pacific Rim region contained countries with some of the fastest growing economies in the world and that the economic climate was impacting on food production, processing and consumption patterns.

Countries that once predominantly consumed rice or tuber based starches as staple food items were diversifying their food intakes dramatically as the standard of living rose in their respective countries. Significantly, this change was resulting in an increase in the consumption of wheat based foods, some traditional products of the region, others new, but adapted to local taste and eating behaviours.

While many of the economies of the Asian part of the Pacific rim region are currently experiencing economic problems, there is little doubt they will recover and the trend towards wheat based food consumption that has commenced will continue. These changes are of significance to us as cereal chemists, as they pose new challenges to adapt existing, and develop new technologies to suit these new and growing markets.

Traditional food consumption trends were documented as the base for examining the changes that were taking place in terms of production and processing technologies. As many of the foods consumed in these countries are different to the breads consumed in western diets, new knowledge on what has been for parts of the region, products consumed for centuries or longer, is essential for us as cereal chemists to meet the food production, processing and distribution challenges that exist in these countries.

The symposium also integrates plant based foods with the use of cereals in animal based food production as there is little doubt that the intensive livestock industries will play an increasingly important role in meeting the demands posed by a growing population on global food production.

Aquaculture production was specially targeted because it is an emerging industry in the Asian region, which is the region of primary focus for the food product range examined in the symposium.

To address these issues a panel of international experts was assembled by invitation. All invitees have responded to the challenge by producing contributions that review and add to the state of our knowledge.

A B Blakeney and L O'Brien

Contents

Changing Cereal Consumption Trends in the Pacific Region

Brian T Oleson
Cooperatives and Group Marketing, University of Manitoba, Winnipeg, Manitoba, Canada (On secondment from the Canadian Wheat Board).

Introduction

Changes in cereal consumption in the Pacific region, as in the rest of the world, are driven by four factors: population, income, tastes and trade policy. While I will elaborate on these driving forces of change in a few moments, I believe it is safe to say that nowhere on the face of this planet is the combined impact of these forces more powerful than they are in the Pacific region. Let me begin with a clarification of the term "Pacific region." Many countries of the Western Hemisphere border the Pacific, and many Asian countries do not. My focus is on south east Asia, including the Indian sub-continent.

Why is this region so important? Very simply, it is because the population is large, the population growth rate is high, and the economic growth rate, until the recent setback, has been astonishing. This means that this region is having and will continue to have a tremendous impact on the world economy and, more specifically, on the Pacific region, or the so-called Pacific Rim countries.

My focus in this paper is on wheat, coarse grains and, to a lesser extent, rice. My projections of wheat and coarse grains are drawn from recent work of the Market Analysis Department at the Canadian Wheat Board as well as other recent long-term studies. Since south east Asia is a large grouping of countries, I will discuss the region as a whole and highlight China, Thailand and Indonesia as case examples.

Asian Cereal Demand in a World Context

For some reason that is not entirely clear, a number of longer-term studies on food security and trade have emerged in recent years. Perhaps these were stimulated by the FAO World Food Summit in November 1996. Perhaps they were stimulated by millennium fever, or perhaps there is increasing recognition of the precarious balance that must be maintained if the world is to somehow successfully navigate its way through the political, demographic and environmental minefields related to food supply and demand over the next few decades.

These studies range from the relative near future (eg. five years) to the more distant future of 2025. If the year 2025 seems far away, consider that a child born in 1998 will only be reaching the youthful age of 27 in the year 2025. I might add that, in most of these studies, grains occupy a central role. The demand for grain, from a grain exporter point of view, is driven by four basic factors: demography, income, tastes and trade/tariff policies.

1. Demography

The most important demographic statistics are the size of a population and its growth rate. Other important considerations that influence demand for cereals are the location of the population, the level of urbanisation, the rate of urbanisation, and the age distribution. For the past half century, it is fair to say that demographic forecasts have been very reliable. A snapshot of current thinking suggests that the world population will be about six billion in the year 2000 and will level off at ten billion by the year 2050.

Quite obviously, population growth will be a major determinant of cereal trends in Asia, which currently accounts for 55 percent of world population and will still account for 48 percent of world population by the year 2050 given these projections. While not within the scope of this paper, it is clear that the most daunting challenge in terms of economic development and food security is that of Africa.

2. Income Growth

The potential demand that is created by population growth is translated into effective demand only if people have the income to buy food. The World Bank projections for income growth in Asia are very high. Growth rates for the United States and Australia are shown for contrast.

Table 1.   **Population Projections to the Year 2050 (billions)**

	1975	2000	2020	2050
World	4.0	6.2	8.0	10.7
Asia	2.2	3.6	4.7	5.2
Japan	0.1	0.1	0.1	0.1
China	0.9	1.3	1.5	1.6
India	0.6	1.0	1.4	1.6
Indonesia	0.1	0.2	0.2	0.3
Africa	0.4	0.8	1.4	2.5

Source: UN World Population Prospects, 1993

The Asian economic crisis triggered in the fall of 1997 provides the basis for well-founded scepticism regarding the accuracy of such long-term projections on income. Clearly the income portion of the growth equation is not nearly so stable or reliable as that of population.

3. Tastes

The combined impact of globalisation, urbanisation and income growth are giving rise to significant changes in the pattern of food demand in many Asian countries. In general, wheat and feed grains will be beneficiaries of these changes. Wheat and wheat products (bread products, noodles, etc.) benefit from urbanisation trends, while coarse grains benefit significantly from income
growth, which drives demand for meat and other coarse-grain-based products, including beer. Both wheat and coarse grain demand seem to benefit from globalisation, which includes the spread of developed-country tastes for value-added wheat-based products, beer and meat. This includes rapid growth for a wide variety of fast foods which, in turn, drives demand for consistent high-quality flours.   On the other hand, per capita consumption of rice shows little change, as is indicated in Table 3. This means that growth in rice consumption is driven mainly by population growth.

Table 2. **Projected Growth in Real Income per Person (percent)**

	1980-93	2000	2010
Australia	1.6	1.7	1.6
United States	1.7	1.9	1.8
Japan	3.4	2.3	2.4
South Korea	8.2	6.3	4.4
China	8.2	9.0	7.2
Indonesia	4.2	6.5	6.9
Philippines	-0.6	2.2	4.4
Thailand	6.4	7.4	6.3
India	3.0	4.2	5.6

Source: World Bank, as reported in Food Security: A Future Perspective

In the above-noted study, growth in per capita coarse grain demand appears modest, with per capita consumption of coarse grains (in developing countries in total) increasing from 40 to 45 kilograms per person by 2016. However, this growth combined with high population growth implies an increase in feed grain use by 67 percent. In Asia, consumption of poultry, dairy, beef and pork will rise with income. Consumption and export of aquaculture products, especially eel, shrimp and some varieties of fish, will expand. This will result in an increased demand for feed grains. As well, beer consumption will increase due to higher per capita consumption and expansion of the tourist trade in this region. However, there are limits to the consumption growth of pork and beer in Islamic areas and of beef in Buddhist and Hindu areas of this region.

4. Tariffs and Trade

In order for consumption and trade to expand beyond domestic production, consumers need access to imported supplies. This is not possible if there are large tariff or non-tariff border measures. The Uruguay Round Agreement provided a framework for agriculture under which domestic support and export subsidies would be reduced and under which market access would be improved. The primary vehicle to accomplish this was the replacement of non-tariff barriers with tariffs (tariffication) and the subsequent reduction of all tariffs.

Table 3. **Projected Annual Per Capita Food Grains Consumption (kilograms)**

	Indonesia		Philippines		China		India	
	1995	2011	1995	2011	1995	2011	1995	2011
Rice	175	195	106	101	105	106	80	91
Wheat	15	28	29	39	87	116	59	77
Coarse Grain	26	28	37	40	29	35	22	24
Total	216	251	173	181	221	257	160	191

Source: Food Security and Trade: A Future Perspective Australia DFAT (1996)

In the final analysis, Asian responses to the Uruguay Round Agreement were very modest. Very little was given up regarding rice, and tariffs after tariffication are still quite high on many agriculture products. However, economic growth in this region has been so dynamic that, while rice is protected and markets are often controlled, there is still considerable scope for growth in wheat, coarse grains, oilseeds and value-added agricultural products. In many cases, imports are growing much faster than consumption. In short, at this time it is the dynamic economies of Asia and not trade reform that are driving import increases in agri-food products. However, the frameworks developed in the Uruguay Round are likely to become increasingly important in future years.

Canadian Wheat Board Forecast of Grain Trade

In 1995, the CWB published projections on the long-term outlook in the report "CWB Grain Trade Forecast to 2005." Recently, this report has been updated with five- and ten-year projections to 2002-03 and 2007-08, respectively. The results for all wheat (including durum), durum, coarse grains (including barley) and barley are displayed in Table 4.

**Table 4.   CWB Grain Trade Forecasts
(million tonnes)**

	Base Period 1992-96	2002-03	2007-08
Wheat	99.9	110.0	125.5
Durum	6.0	7.0	8.0
Coarse Grain	90.0	104.5	123.3
Barley	15.4	18.0	20.1
- Malting Barley	2.9	3.7	4.6

Source: CWB Grain Trade Forecast to 2005.

**Table 5.   CWB Grain Import Forecast for Asia
(million tonnes)**

	Base Period 1992-96	2002-03	2007-08
Wheat	32	40	46
Coarse Grain	42	50	58

Source: CWB Grain Trade Forecast to 2005.

World wheat trade is projected to increase from about 100 million tonnes to 125 million tonnes. The Asian share of this trade is forecast to increase from 32 to 36 percent. A very bright spot in this study is Indonesia, which is projected to increase wheat imports to 8 million tonnes by 2007, making it one of the world's largest importers of wheat.

China is the wild card. Imports of wheat by China are projected at 9 million tonnes in 2002 and 12 million tonnes in 2007. This is in the middle of the range of the various studies. Reasonable changes in assumptions produce radically different outcomes. At one extreme, China could be a minor exporter of wheat. At the other extreme, Chinese demand literally overwhelms the world wheat trade.

With respect to coarse grain, trade is projected to increase from 90 million tonnes in the base period to 123 million tonnes by 2007. This study, I should note, takes a much more bullish or buoyant view of world coarse grain trade than the earlier CWB study, which forecast little growth to the year 2005. The question of world coarse grain trade is closely linked to the question of world meat trade. Asia's share of coarse grain trade is projected to increase slightly. One segment where Asian demand is projected to increase rapidly is malting barley.

Cereal Consumption Trends in Selected Countries

China

China is generally thought of as a rice-consuming country. However, vast geographical area results in very different food patterns in different regions of the country. Generally speaking, rice is the staple for southern China and wheat is the predominant grain in northern China. At present, China's total rice consumption is 132 million tonnes, and its annual per capita consumption 105-110 kilograms. Total consumption for wheat is 113 million tonnes and per capita consumption is over 90 kilograms. China will likely increase its wheat consumption at least as fast as its growth in population (that alone would increase consumption 1.35 million tonnes per year, given the same level of per capita wheat consumption as present). Chinese per capita wheat consumption is quite high by world and North American standards – higher than Canada's and on a par with that of the U.S. It may be a "mature" market in terms of per capita wheat consumption, ie. one with little potential for further growth on a per capita basis in large parts of the country. This is the conclusion of the Canadian Wheat Board study. However, the study acknowledges that income growth and diet improvement in rural areas and an increase in wheat-based value-added products in large metropolitan centers leave room for slow growth for per capita wheat consumption. On this basis, the CWB projects that China's per capita consumption will reach 95 kilograms by 2002, and 98 kilograms by 2007. This is much more modest than the 123 kilograms projected by the Australian Department of Foreign Affairs and Trade study.

Malting barley demand is determined by total beer consumption. The beer industry in China has been growing quite rapidly in recent years. There is still significant room for growth in beer consumption. Annual per capita beer consumption in China is 13 litres, compared with the European average of 80 litres. Total beer output capacity reached 16.4 million tonnes in 1996. China is currently the world's second-largest beer producer, just behind the United States, and is predicted to be the largest beer producer within a few years.

**Table 6.   Consumption Growth in China
               (percent)**

	Growth 1980-95	Growth 1990-95
Wheat	3.0	0.4
Vegetables	9.2	9.4
Fruit	10.3	12.6
Beef	19.0	30.3
Pork	7.9	9.7
Chicken	13.1	22.2
Dairy	8.0	6.1

Source: R. Barichello. "Asian Adaptation to Gatt"
               "From Gatt to the WTO" conference. October 27-28, 1997.
               Saskatoon, Canada.

On balance, the per capita utilisation of grain for food is likely to remain fairly stable, while per capita utilisation of grain for feed will continue to increase.

The following table shows that the growth rate for livestock products over the past fifteen years was very high, and the growth rate was even higher for the past five years.

Thailand

Like most other south east Asian countries, Thailand is a rice-producing country. It is the second-largest rice exporter in the world. The annual domestic consumption of rice is about 8.6 million tonnes, while annual per capita consumption is about 144 kilograms.

In contrast, per capita wheat consumption in Thailand is only 9 kilograms.

However, closer examination reveals that, while total rice consumption has been increasing since the early 1960s due to population growth, per capita consumption has been steadily decreasing. On the other hand, per capita wheat consumption is on the rise, growing about 7.5 percent per year since 1980. Rising incomes, the increasing popularity of convenience foods and growth in tourism point to continued expansion of wheat-based foods. Thailand's current annual per capita wheat consumption is about 10 kilograms. Further growth is likely if the current duty on wheat imports is reduced or removed.

Indonesia

Indonesia's staple food is rice. Both the total consumption and per capita consumption of rice have been increasing steadily. Per capita consumption of rice is about 170 kilograms.

Indonesia does not produce wheat, and therefore imports all that is consumed. Imports last year were 4.2 million tonnes, and are projected to increase to 4.5 million tonnes in 1997-98. Given its large population of 207 million, consumption for wheat is still relatively low, in spite of its large import program. However, consumption of wheat is increasing at an astonishing rate. Annual per capita consumption was only 19 kilograms in 1996, and is projected to increase to 22 kilograms this year. Average annual per capita consumption growth in the years between 1992 and 1996 was 7.8 percent, and the growth rate for 1997 is expected to reach 10 percent. Trend growth in consumption since 1985 led the CWB to predict that imports of wheat might reach 8 million tonnes by 2007. This implies that per capita wheat consumption will surpass 25 kilograms within ten years, an impressive record for a country with no history of wheat production or culture of wheat consumption.

The increase in wheat demand can be attributed to several factors. Indonesia's population is growing at 1.7 percent annually, and is projected to grow to 241 million by 2007. As well, until the recent economic crisis in the region, the Indonesian economy was booming: average annual growth in GDP was 7 percent in the 1990s. Prior to the recent economic crisis, World Bank projections for Indonesian growth were in the range of

7.5 percent to 8 percent over the next ten years. Increasing income and availability of imports have made it possible for people to diversify consumption to include non-traditional foods. The demand for convenience foods, especially instant noodles, is growing rapidly. In short, changing dietary patterns are boosting Indonesian demand for wheat-based products. There is also an increasing number of U.S.-based franchises of restaurants and fast-food outlets that cater both to growing Indonesian demand and to demand from the rising number of tourists.

Table 7.   Consumption Growth in Indonesia
(percent)

	Growth 1980-95	Growth 1990-95
Wheat	7.2	14.4
Vegetables	5.5	5.4
Fruit	2.7	2.5
Beef	5.0	14.3
Pork	9.1	3.7
Chicken	11.7	12.4
Dairy	1.7	12.1

Source: R. Barichello. "Asian Adaptation to Gatt"
"From Gatt to the WTO" conference. October 27-28, 1997.
Saskatoon, Canada.

Similar to other newly-industrialising countries in Asia, the increased standard of living in Indonesia has increased demand for other high-value foods besides wheat. Indonesia's livestock industry is projected to continue to grow rapidly. The growth rate for beef consumption averaged 5 percent per year since 1980, while the annual growth rate for the past five years has jumped to 14.3 percent. The annual growth rate in consumption of both poultry and dairy is over 12 percent for the past five years. This rapid growth in livestock, dairy and poultry has, in turn, supported rapid growth in the animal feed industry. Corn is the major feed grain produced in Indonesia. Corn consumption has been increasing at an average annual rate of 6 percent in the 1990s, up from 4 percent in the 1980s. In 1996-97, total consumption of corn will be about 7.3 million tonnes.

Concluding Comments

Rapid population increase, urbanisation, buoyant economic growth, globalisation of communication, commerce and technology, and liberalisation of trade are rapidly altering the food landscape of most Asian economies. Diet is being diversified. There is always a danger that the current economic crisis will lead to prolonged or chronic recession or depression. Barring this scenario, there will continue to be a rapid expansion in the demand for wheat-based products, beer, poultry, pork, beef, dairy and a myriad of other agriculture products. For wheat and coarse grains, this means greater demand over the next decade, and it also means a greater emphasis on quality. There will be immense pressure on the scientific community to develop high-yielding, high-performance grains. This must be achieved in an environment where increasing emphasis will be placed on cost effectiveness, the environment and sustainability. It is a challenge well worthy of the efforts of us all.

References

Canadian Wheat Board. "CWB Grain Trade Forecast to 2004-05." Winnipeg, 1995. (Revised version to 2007-08 is forthcoming.)

Commonwealth of Australia, Department of Foreign Affairs and Trade. Food Security – A Future Perspective. Canberra, 1996.

Food and Agricultural Policy Research Institute (FAPRI). FAPRI U.S. Agricultural Outlook. Ames IA and Columbia MO, 1993.

International Food Policy Research Institute (IFPRI). World Supply and Demand Projections for Cereals, 2020. Washington, 1994.

International Policy Council on Agriculture Food and Trade. Attaining Global Food Security by 2025. Position Paper No. 3. Washington, 1996.

Barichello, R. "Asian Adaptation to GATT: Prospects for Agricultural Trade." Saskatoon, 1997.

Huang, J., S. Rozelle and M. W. Rosegrant. "China's Food Economy to the Twenty-First Century: Supply Demand and Trade." IFPRI Discussion Paper. Washington, 1997.

International Food Policy Research Institute (IFPRI). Population and Food in the Early Twenty-First Century. Washington, 1995.

Traditional and changing food consumption trends for wheat based foods

Seiichi Nagao
Wheat Flour Institute, Flour Millers Association, Tokyo, Japan

Introduction

The traditional and current situation of wheat based foods in the diet of people in the Pacific region is unique and different for each area. In areas where people live in Western culture such as USA, Canada, Australia and New Zealand, breads and rolls have been the main carbohydrate sources. On the other hand, rice rather than wheat is the traditional staple food in most Asian countries. Wheat, however, is one of the main caloric sources of people in northern China, and some amount of unique wheat based foods such as noodles, steamed breads and dumplings have been traditionally eaten in almost all areas of eastern Asia. So not only have wheat based foods been traditionally consumed but also consumption in the forms of Western foods is becoming more and more common each year.

In the regions of Western culture

Breads and rolls have been traditionally eaten at every meal in the regions of Western culture. Their consumption was very high in the past, but a part of them was replaced by a variety of other delicious foods including meats, vegetables and fruits. Cakes, biscuits, cookies and crackers are traditional confectioneries liked by many. The consumption of pasta in the form of dry, frozen and refrigerated products is increasing in those areas, and they have potential to expand their market. People began to accept other wheat based foods introduced from other parts of the world including Asian noodles in their dietary life, though consumption is still very limited. Breakfast cereals are very popular as a carbohydrate source for breakfast, but wheat is not the main material of these products.

It is my understanding that the consumption of breads and rolls in Australia and New Zealand is still at a rather low level compared with that in the past and shows little sign of increase. I sincerely hope that wheat flour consumption in Australia and New Zealand will increase as soon as possible through cooperative work within the wheat industry as well as intensive efforts by each company.

Figure 1 shows the change of annual flour consumption per capita in the USA The lowest figure was 49.9 kg. in 1972. Since then, it has increased steadily. In 1996, 67.1 kg of wheat flour was consumed per person, which was almost equal to that in the UK and the total cereal consumption in France and Germany. As the amount is still not large compared with the total cereal consumption in most areas of eastern Asia, it is expected to increase further in the future. There is no doubt that the increased consumption of wheat flour has contributed to the improved condition of people's health in the USA Several reasons are provided to explain the current upward trend of flour consumption. Following the issuing of dietary guidelines by the Government, people began to eat more breads and rolls than before in place of eating too much beef. Many varieties of improved quality breads and rolls, including high fibre breads are now displayed on the shelves of supermarkets and food stores. The development of various types of attractive fast food chains including bagel, pizza, tortilla and pasta shops is offering consumers many opportunities for eating more flour products. The increase in the Hispanic and Asian population is also activating the market for wheat based foods. Flour tortilla is expanding its market and currently, eastern Asian food, particularly Asian noodle, is a trendy cuisine among some consumers. Asian noodles include *lo mein* (made from egg and wheat flour), *udon, soba* (made from buckwheat flour and wheat flour) and *ramen* (Chinese type noodle made from hard wheat flour in Japan). Summarising these trends, the USA is thought to be a very promising market for wheat based foods, but continuous effort has to be expended to maintain and increase the future consumption of wheat based foods.

In the regions of Asian culture

Annual per capita wheat consumption in China is about 86 kg, which is almost equal to that in North America. However, it was only 20 kg in 1950, and a dramatic increase took place in the 1970s. It is estimated that 75 to 80% of wheat flour is used for steamed breads, noodles and dumplings, 13 to 18% for confectioneries including cakes and cookies, and 7 to 8% for

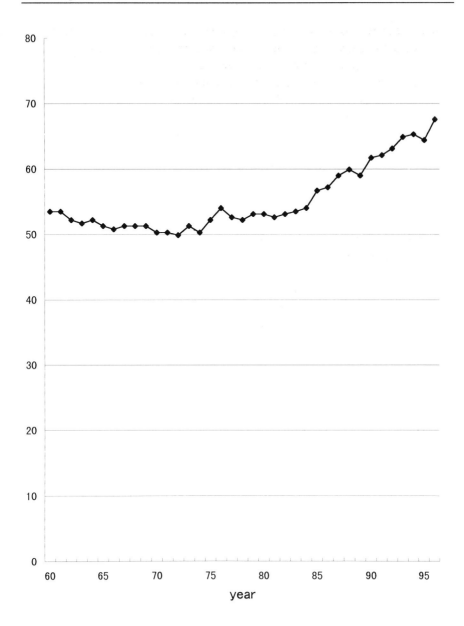

Figure 1. Wheat flour consumption per capita per annum (kg) in the USA

breads and rolls. Wheat, an important crop next to rice in China is mainly produced in the northern part of the Yellow River. In northern China, a large amount of steamed breads have been traditionally eaten at every meal as a staple food and about 70% of wheat flour consumed in this area is eaten in the form of steamed breads. Noodles occupy about 20 to 30% of meals consumed in northern China.

Nan, a type of flat bread, is a staple food in some north-western areas of China. Wheat gluten torn and fried in vegetable oil is a material for soup, stew and other dishes. Rice has been the staple food in southern China, but noodles occupy about 15% of meals. Dumplings with chopped pork as filling were eaten on special occasions such as festivals and the entertainment of guests in the past, but are now very popular in daily meals. Boiled type dumplings are most popular among the boiled, steamed and baked products. Breads and rolls containing 6 to 15% of sugar in the formula are becoming popular in China, especially in urban areas and the consumption of instant noodles is increasing year by year in southern China. Though the ash content of most wheat flours produced in China is very high, some premium flours, which contain a little less ash than ordinary flour, are now sold in urban markets. As the standard of living is improved, a variety of wheat based foods will be produced and eaten in China, which is the most promising market for increased consumption of wheat based products.

In other parts of eastern Asia, little wheat based foods were eaten in the past, but consumption is now increasing in conjunction with an improvement in the standard of living and the introduction of Western culture. In South Korea, wheat flour consumption per capita per annum was 34.5 kg in 1995, which fluctuated between 32.1 and 39.5 kg since 1980. About 63% of wheat flour milled in South Korea is classified as all-purpose flour, which is mainly used for making noodles. In 1995, 47.5% of flour was used for noodles, 21.8% was for breads, rolls and confectioneries, 4.1% was for family use, and 3.2% was for soy sauce production.

Though rice is the staple food in Indonesia, wheat flour consumption has been increasing. Wheat imports in 2000 are estimated to become 4,500,000 tonnes, which amounts to a 5% increase each year. Instant noodles have become the second staple food next to rice in Indonesia. The wheat flour market in the Philippines is growing and becoming quality conscious. Flour millers in the Philippines are trying to import quality wheat from different sources and produce a variety of quality wheat flours to meet the requirements of their customers. In Thailand, wheat flour consumption per capita per annum is only 8 to 9 kg, while that of rice is 120 to 130 kg. However, an increase in people's income, the introduction and spread of convenience foods, an increase in tourists from overseas, etc., will bring about a gradual expansion in the sale of wheat based foods in the future. The current percentage of wheat flour used in Thailand is about 30% for shrimp feed, 20% for breads, 20% for noodles, 15% for all-purpose uses, and 15% for biscuits and crackers. Thailand is becoming a quality conscious market. Two flour milling companies which have introduced Japanese milling technology seem to be playing a role to activate the market. Generally speaking, however, the recent economic depression spread over the region has slowed the upward trend in the consumption of wheat based foods.

Japan as a unique and leading market

In Japan, wheat flour consumption per capita for food use in 1995 was 32.8 kg, while that of pearled rice was 67.8 kg. At the beginning of this century, the consumption of rice was more than double the current amount, and that of wheat flour was less than one-tenth the current figure. Traditionally, people in Japan have been omnivorous. Although rice was the staple food for them in the past, they have always eaten a small amount of wheat and other cereals. White salted (*udon*) noodles, including hand-made dried noodles and some confectioneries such as steamed or baked buns have been eaten at special occasions for more than 1,000 years. However, their consumption was very limited until the turn of this century. As shown in Figure 2, wheat flour production in 1910 was only 400,000 tonnes. In those days, the greater part of wheat flour consumed was in the form of white salted noodles, but some people living in urban areas began to eat breads, rolls, cakes and biscuits.

Since the 1950s, wheat flour consumption has increased considerably year by year, and reached approximately 5,000,000 tonnes in 1996. It would be significant to look back on the big change in the dietary life of the Japanese and the rapid growth of wheat flour industry in the past 50 years. Long and oval rolls which children ate for school lunch played an important part in the introduction of breads and rolls to people's daily meals. The mass production of white square pan bread at moderate prices by newly opened large bakeries was another epoch-making contribution to the increase in bread consumption. The shape of the bread was almost similar to that sold in North America, but its crumb texture was quite unique. Its soft, moist and silky texture was welcomed by a majority of consumers who were accustomed to the sticky taste of boiled rice.

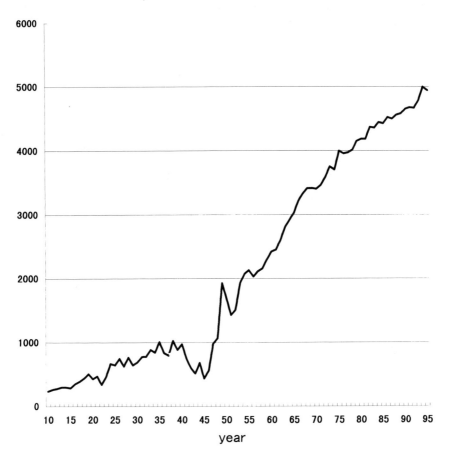

Figure 2. Wheat flour production in Japan (1,000 tonnes)

Many modern large bakery plants were built one after another in the 1960s. They learned and introduced a variety of delicious breads and rolls from Western Europe and North America. Some of the introduced breads and rolls retained their original appearance and taste, but others were modified to meet the unique preferences of the local consumers. Convenient toasters developed by electric companies helped to replace one or two bowls of boiled rice with two or three slices of toasted bread for breakfast.

Now, people are enjoying sandwiches, hamburgers, hot dogs, doughnuts and sweetened buns for lunch and snacks. A variety of rolls and buns with curry, tuna paste, salad, mashed potato, *chow mein* or croquette as a filling are very popular among the young for their lunch and for snacks. Harmonisation of traditional Japanese life style with introduced Western culture has also promoted the consumption of breads and rolls in many different places and ways. Current consumption of breads and rolls in Japan is about 12 kg of wheat flour per head per annum. This figure is not so large compared with that in Western countries, but breads and rolls have established a position as a staple food co-existing with boiled rice and a variety of noodles. So many different kinds of breads, rolls and buns varying in shape and taste and based on English, French, German, Austrian, Italian, Danish, Swedish, American, Arabic, Chinese and Japanese types are now enjoyed by consumers, enriching their dietary life.

Noodles are traditional foods in Japan and a sharp increase in consumption occurred after the 1950s as was the case for breads and rolls. It is considered that improvement in the standard of living was the most significant factor contributing to the increase of noodle consumption. Wheat flour production for noodle use including pasta in 1995 was 1,747,000 tonnes, which comprised 35.3% of total flour production. Table 1 shows the types of noodles now produced in Japan.

The development of an instant noodle in 1960 was an epoch-making event. In the beginning, quality of instant noodles was less than satisfactory, but through research and development their quality has been improved and many attractive new products have been developed. Instant noodles are now one of the main type of noodles consumed. In 1995, 314,000 tonnes of instant noodles were produced, of which snack type cup noodles comprised

Table 1. Types of noodles produced in Japan

Main group	Subgroup & type[a]	
Uncooked wet & Boiled noodles	White salted noodles (*Udon*)	Fresh
		Boiled
	Chinese type noodles (*Ramen)*	Fresh
		Boiled
		Steamed
	Buckwheat noodles (*Soba*)	Fresh
		Boiled
	Thin dough pieces for dumplings	(*Gyoza*)
		(*Wonton*)
		(*Shumai*)
		(*Harumaki*)
Dried noodles	Flat noodles (*Hira-men*)	
	Udon)	Machine-made
		Handmade
	Thin noodles (*Hiya-mugi*)	Machine-made
		Handmade
	Very thin noodles (*So-men*)	Machine-made
		Handmade
	Buckwheat noodles	
	Chinese type noodles	
Instant noodles	Chinese style	Fried
		Non-fried
	Japanese style	Fried
		Non-fried
Pasta	Long type	Spaghetti
		Noodle
		Vermicelli
	Short type	Macaroni
		Shell
	Special type	Alphabet
		Farfalla
Others	Rice noodles	
	Starch noodles	

[a]Japanese names in parentheses

147,000 tonnes, Chinese type noodles comprised 163,000 tonnes and

Japanese type noodles comprised 4,000 tonnes. Instant noodles are mainly eaten as snacks and for lunch.

The production of white salted *udon* type noodles excluding the instant type was 480,000 tonnes in 1995, in which the ratio of fresh to dried types was 45 to 55. The market for fresh type *udon* noodles is still expanding, whereas the consumption of dried type noodles has been stable since the late 1970s. Combined research and development effort by the noodle industries has resulted in quality improvement enabling the production of new attractive products and new delicious noodle dishes. The use of frozen noodle technology has enabled delicious boiled noodles to be served in a short time leading to an increase in fresh noodle consumption. Access to a constant supply of quality noodle wheat suitable for *udon* noodle production from Western Australia has been a major contributing factor to the development of these products and increased noodle consumption. Among dried type white salted noodles the market for tasty handmade type products is expanding.

The increase in noodle consumption indicates that quality improvement, development of new attractive products and introduction of new ways of cooking and eating are so important even in the case of traditional foods. Manufacturers have to continually strive to supply attractive products to meet the preference of their customers in cooperation with suppliers and marketers.

The consumption of pasta is also increasing annually in most areas of the Pacific region, and is expected to continue.

So many kinds of traditional and newly introduced confectioneries based on wheat flour as shown in Table 2 are sold in the Japanese market. They are roughly classified into Japanese, Chinese and Western types. Some of them are traditional products, but others are products introduced from many parts of the world and modified to meet the taste of local consumers. Now, if you happened to walk around a large city in Japan, you would be able to see almost all kinds of flour based confectioneries originating from all over the world, which are contributing to the happy and varied food life of local people.

Table 2. Wheat Flour Confectioneries in Japan

Main group	Subgroup	Item[a]
Baked goods	Biscuits	Hard biscuit
		Soft biscuit
		Cookie
		Cracker
	Baked small goods	*Saga*[b]*-bolo*
		Soba-bolo
	Japanese cracknels	Tile-shaped cracknel (*Kawara-senbei*)
		Nanbu cracknel (*Nanbu*[b]*-senbei*)
	Wafers	Wafer
Fried goods	Doughnuts	Cake doughnuts
		Yeast doughnuts
	Fried dough cookies	*Karintou*
Fresh Japanese-style goods	Lightly baked buns	Chestnut bun with bean jam filling (*Kuri-manju*)
		Bean jam pancake (*Dora-yaki*)
		Japanese muffin with bean jam filling (*Imagawa-yaki, tai-yaki*)
	Steamed buns	Leavened bun (*Saka-mauju*)
		Chemically leavened bun (*Mushi-manju*)
Fresh Western-style goods	Castilla	Nagasaki[b]*-castilla*
	Cakes	Sponge cake
		Butter cake
		Waffle
		Hot cake
		Chou a la crème
		Baumkuchen
Fresh Chinese-style goods	Steamed buns	Chinese bun with bean jam filling (*An-manju*)
		Chinese bun with meat filling (*Niku-manju*)

[a]Japanese names in parentheses
[b]Names of locations (city, area, region, etc.)

Conclusions

Wheat flour is a very important raw material in the production of staple foods and snacks as well as for cooking. It serves to maintain the carbohydrate intake of consumers at an ideal level. It is an indispensable raw material for the production of convenient, instant, fashionable products, hence it contributes significantly to the happy, delicious and healthy dietary life of consumers. The current dietary profile of the Japanese is generally thought to be ideal for the maintenance of a healthy and long life span. Foods eaten every day include a modified mixture of Japanese, Chinese and Western foods and dishes, and comprise so many kinds of food materials including cereals, other starchy materials, beans, meat, milk, chicken, eggs, fishes, shellfishes, vegetables, mushrooms, seaweeds, fruits, tea, etc. In the processing and cooking of many of these foods wheat flour plays an important role. The delicate taste and preference of Japanese consumers demands the production of wheat flours suitable for the manufacture of each product. This results in Japanese flour millers producing many kinds of high quality wheat flours by managing sophisticated flour milling technology in order to meet the requirements of their customers.

We can safely say that wheat based foods are leading contributors to the happy and healthy dietary life of Japan. However, it remains necessary to monitor the current and changing trend of wheat based foods in the other parts of the world and to actively introduce and adapt from them potential new products for Japanese consumers. In order to give consumers more variation and satisfaction in their dietary life, wheat based foods suitable for each meal as well as tasty snack foods eaten at any time and place continually need to be developed. Further improvement in quality, manufacturing process and technology has to be pursued in order to be able to offer more delicious and variable foods. Development of delicious wheat based foods which are easily eaten with other nutritious foods, along with enrichment of functional nutrients in the products will help to meet consumer's demands for healthy food products. The cooperation of wheat suppliers in Australia, the USA and Canada is also very important for the supply of safe and quality wheat based foods to consumers. I hope wheat based foods will play an important role in the happy and healthy dietary life of people in the Pacific region.

Rice based convenience foods

Ken'ichi Ohtsubo
National Food Research Institute, Ministry of Agriculture, Forestry and Fisheries, Tsukuba Science City, Ibaraki, Japan

Along with wheat and corn, rice is one of the most important cereals in the world. Globally, more than 500 million tonnes of paddy rice are produced each year with about 90% of it being produced and consumed in the densely-populated Asian countries where it is a staple food item.

Besides being consumed directly as food, rice is processed and utilised in various kinds of foodstuffs. Examples of processed rice products include parboiled rice, fermented rice wine, rice noodles, rice crackers, rice cakes, rice snacks, rice flour and other fermented rice products.

Processed rice products in Japan are shown in Figure 1. In 1995, according to the Ministry of Agriculture, Forestry and Fisheries of Japan, 9,115,000 tonnes of rice were used for staple food as cooked rice, 490,000 tonnes for Sake wine fermentation, 233,000 tonnes for rice cracker and rice flour production and 100,000 tonnes for Miso fermentation.

This paper introduces some of the convenience based foods manufactured from rice.

1. Traditional rice based convenience foods in Japan

One of the most famous traditional rice based convenience foods in Japan is "Sushi". Sushi originated as a preservative food for fish using natural fermentation ("Narezushi") with the cooked rice being used as the substrate along with salt for *Lactobacillus* bacteria. "Nigirizushi" was developed in Tokyo in the 1800's as an easy to prepare rice dish, made by pressing a cooked rice ball manually and topped with sliced raw fish.

Cooked rice becomes more tasty with the addition of salt, sugar and vinegar after cooking. Soy sauce and grated horse radish ("wasabi") are necessary to enjoy the original taste of "Sushi".

"Onigiri" or "Omusubi" is another traditional rice based convenience food in Japan. These cooked rice balls wrapped with bamboo leaves were used as a lunch box for many years (Figure 2).

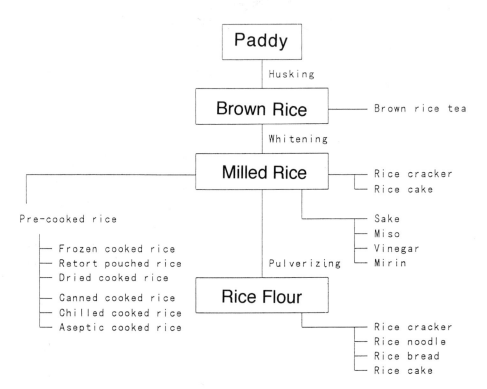

Figure 1. Processed rice products in Japan.

2. Breakfast cereals from rice

Rice based breakfast cereals are made from rice grains, milled rice flours or cooked rice dough. These rice materials are pre-cooked, dried, flaked and then expanded or puffed and toasted. Examples of these products are puffed rice, rice flakes and shredded rice cereals. Various kinds of breakfast cereals were developed in the USA, China, Korea, Thailand, Vietnam and many other Pacific countries.

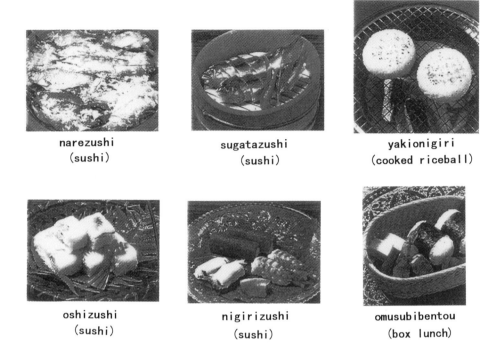

| narezushi
(sushi) | sugatazushi
(sushi) | yakionigiri
(cooked riceball) |
| oshizushi
(sushi) | nigirizushi
(sushi) | omusubibentou
(box lunch) |

Figure 2. Traditional rice based convenience foods in Japan.

3. Retort Rice

Retort rice was developed in the early 1970's in Japan. Rice and water are packed in a laminated plastic container and pasteurised at 120°C. To consume the product, purchasers can either soak it in hot water for 15 min or heat it in a microwave oven for 1 min. The shelf life of this product is half a year without refrigeration and the price is reasonable. The problems with this product are off-flavours developed by the excess heating and texture of the cooked rice grains. Twenty two thousand tonnes of retort rice was produced in Japan in 1996.

4. Canned rice

Canned rice has been produced for more than 50 years. Milled rice and water is placed in tin cans, steamed for 30 min and sealed and sterilised in a retort at 112°C for 80 min. The product is consumed after heating it in hot water for 15 min. The advantage of this product is its long shelf life being able to be stored for several years under natural room conditions.

5. Pre-gelatinised rice

Cooked and dried rice, or pre-gelatinised rice is prepared by the usual method of cooking in water followed by abrupt drying. As its moisture content is very low, it can be preserved for several years under natural conditions. For the consumer, this product is easy to cook as its starch is pre-gelatinised and prevented from retrogradation.

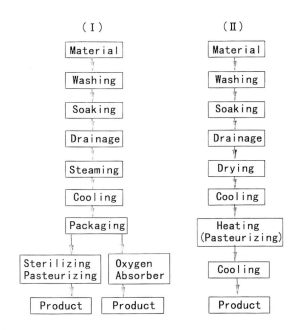

Figure 3. Production procedure for "Quick-cooking Rice".

Instant rice, such as "Cup Rice", is a form of high-quality pre-gelatinised rice. Consumers can eat it by adding only hot water and it keeping warm for several minutes.

Recently, pre-gelatinised and packaged rice without excess drying has been developed in Japan ("Hayadakimai" or "Quick cooking rice"). The procedure by which it is produced is shown in Figure 3. Consumers only have to add to the envelope tasty cooking soup or water and cook for about 15 minutes. They can omit the time-consuming processes of washing the rice, soaking and keeping it warm after cooking. Compared with "Instant rice", quick cooking rice has improved taste and texture. Although its moisture content is more than 35%, it can be stored for several months without refrigeration by pasteurisation or by using an oxygen absorber. Quality evaluation of these various kinds of quick cooking rice, sensory tests, gelatinisation properties, and physical property measurements were conducted in our laboratory in collaborative research with a food industry company, QP Co. Ltd. (Figures 4 and 5).

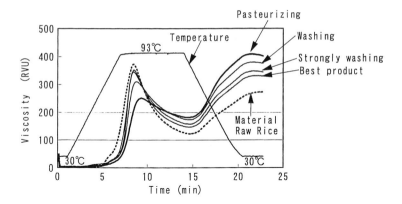

Figure 4. Gelatinisation properties of various "Quick-cooking Rices" and their raw material rice.

6. Frozen cooked rice

The market for frozen cooked rice in Japan expanding to 138,000 tonnes in 1996. Frozen cooked rice is convenient to cook in a microwave oven and its high quality is preserved in a freezer for a long period. It is a rather expensive product but frozen roasted cooked rice balls or frozen pilaf is very popular with Japanese consumers.

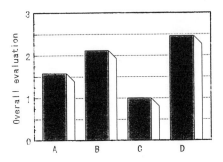

Figure 5a. Results of sensory tests of various "Quick-cooking Rices".
A: Washed   B: Strongly washed   C: Pasteurised   D:Best product

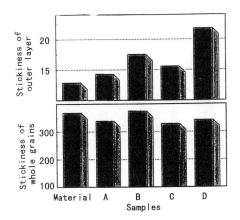

Figure 5b. Stickiness of "Quick-cooking Rice" grains (measured with a Tensipresser).
A: Washed   B: Strongly washed   C: Pasteurised   D: Best product
Outer layer : 25% of compression ratio
Whole grain : 90% of compression ratio

The typical procedure to manufacture frozen cooked rice is shown in Figure 6. In cooperative research with a manufacturer, Mayekawa Co. Ltd, we developed the new freezing technique, "medium rate freezing" for frozen cooked rice balls. Frozen cooked rice balls prepared at the medium freezing rate had better palatability compared with those frozen at the slow or quick rate (Figure 7). Furthermore, its physical properties of hardness and stickiness were better maintained (Figure 8).

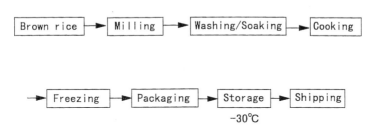

Figure 6. Production procedure for Frozen Cooked Rice.

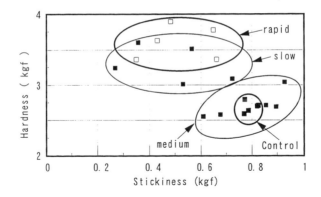

Figure 7. Change in texture of cooked rice grains due to freezing condition (measured with a Texturometer).

7. Aseptic cooked rice

Aseptic cooked rice was developed within one decade in Japan. Rice grains are washed well to remove any bacteria followed by cooking and packaging in a clean broth. As contamination by microorganisms is very low, this product can be stored for half a year under natural room conditions. As the rice is not heated excessively during production, the eating quality of the final product is very good.

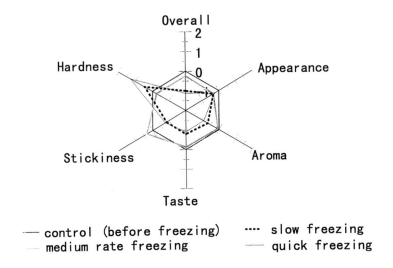

― control (before freezing)   ···· slow freezing
――― medium rate freezing   ――――― quick freezing

Figure 8. Results of sensory tests of Frozen Cooked Rice after different freezing conditions.

8. Cooked rice distributed at low temperature

Cooked rice is packaged in a plastic container and shipped and distributed at temperatures lower than 18°C. This product has some advantages from the viewpoint of sanitation but the problem is the retrogradation of the cooked rice starch. Despite this problem, the market is expanding annually.

9. Rice cracker

There are two types of rice crackers, the glutinous rice cracker ("arare", "kakimochi") and the non-glutinous type ("senbei"). In the case of the high quality rice cracker, "arare", waxy rice is steamed, pounded (or kneaded), refrigerated, cut and baked and then packaged. The quality is affected by the variety of rice, kneading conditions and the refrigeration procedure. The results of research conducted by Dr Watanabe are shown in Table 1 and Figures 9 and 10.

Table 1. The ratio of viscosity to elasticity of rice cakes made from different rice cultivars.

Cultivar	η/J s
Koganemochi	1.19×10^8
Hiyokumochi	1.34×10^8
Tannemochi	2.53×10^8

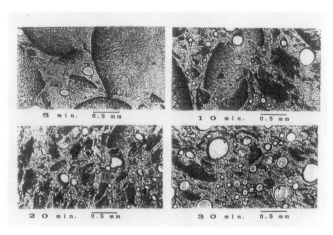

Figure 9. Micrographs of sections of rice cakes made from Koganemochi after different kneading times.

10. Utilisation of pressurisation on rice processing

High pressure treatment was applied to the manufacturing of the rice cracker, rice cake. It is well known that rice crackers are made using many processing steps. High pressure treatment made it possible to simplify the manufacturing process (Figure 11). According to Dr Yamazaki, Echigoseika Co. Ltd, starch of non-glutinous rice was gelatinised by the high pressure treatment of 700 MP at 35°C.

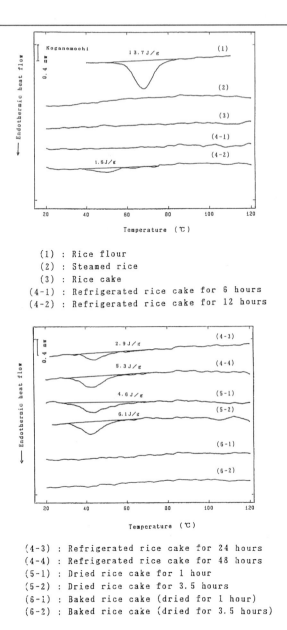

(1) : Rice flour
(2) : Steamed rice
(3) : Rice cake
(4-1) : Refrigerated rice cake for 6 hours
(4-2) : Refrigerated rice cake for 12 hours

(4-3) : Refrigerated rice cake for 24 hours
(4-4) : Refrigerated rice cake for 48 hours
(5-1) : Dried rice cake for 1 hour
(5-2) : Dried rice cake for 3.5 hours
(6-1) : Baked rice cake (dried for 1 hour)
(6-2) : Baked rice cake (dried for 3.5 hours)

Figure 10. DSC curves of various products in the manufacturing process for rice crackers.

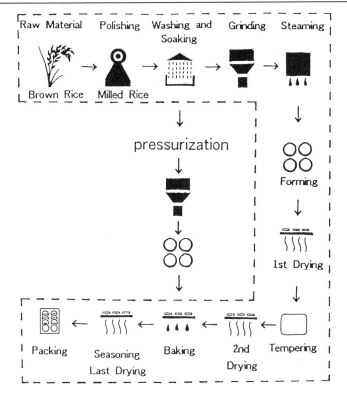

Flow sheet for manufacturing rice crackers.
Dotted line indicates the normal process.

Figure 11. Utilisation of pressurisation in rice processing (courtesy of Dr A Yamazaki of Echigoseika Co. Ltd.).

He also succeeded in developing low allergenic rice which is useful for the preparation of "low allergenic cooked rice" (Figure 12). These rice products are promising because there are many people who are allergic to rice based products.

low allergenic rice bread   low allergenic cooked rice

Figure 12. Low allergenic rice products.

11. Miscellaneous convenience rice products

In south-east Asian countries, such as Thailand, Vietnam, Taiwan and China, rice noodles are very popular convenience foods. High amylose rice is more suitable for the preparation of noodle.

Various kinds of rice products for take away food shops are popular, such as lunch-box, sushi, bamboo-leaf wrapped rice, rice burgers, rice cakes, rice bread and oil-fried rice products.

Modern Noodle Based Foods - Product Range and Production Methods

T. P. Wu, W. Y. Kuo, M. C. Cheng
China Grain Product and Research Development Institute.
Taipei, Taiwan. R. O. C.

Introduction

Noodles are one of the staple foods of the Orient, and noodle consumption is now on the rise throughout Japan, Taiwan, mainland China, and south east Asia. Taiwan imports approximately 900,000 tonnes of wheat annually, and more than one-third of the flour made from this wheat is used as the raw material for noodles. In Taiwan, economic development, changes in lifestyle, and shifts in the family structure have strongly affected eating habits. As far as noodle products are concerned, a range of products once limited to raw and dry noodles has gradually expanded to include a host of derivative products meeting the needs of modern urban consumers. Among these are:

(1) Instant noodles - Deep fried / Non-fried
(2) Dry steamed noodles
(3) Frozen and chilled noodles
(4) Long Life noodles - Acidified / Non-acidified

The manufacturing methods of these products include four common features:

(1) All are mass produced on an economically-efficient scale.
(2) Their front-end (raw noodle) manufacturing process is not greatly different from that of ordinary raw noodles.
(3) There have been no major improvements in front-end processing technology and equipment in recent years.
(4) Chief differences between the various products in terms of processing methods and technologies are found in the back-end.

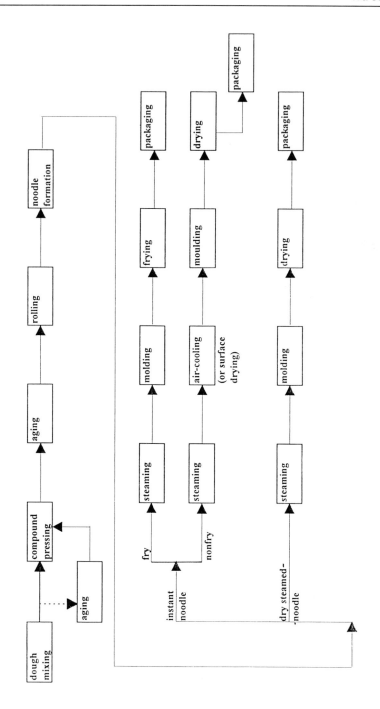

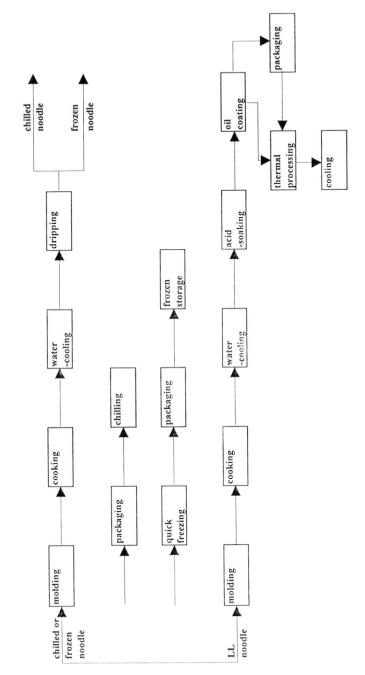

Figure 1. Flow sheets of modern noodle processing.

An Introduction to Processing Methods and Technologies

Figure 1 shows a process flow chart for modern noodle manufacture. Table 1 lists types of products and their commercial characteristics. Because front-end processing is largely the same, front-end processing technology and recent technological advances will be described first.

1. Dough mixing - the vacuum mixing technique with sufficient mixing moisture

When noodles are made by machine via constant-pressure mixing, the need to maintain the hardness of the sheeted dough and insure that the dough does not adhere to the rollers during sheeting necessitates that water added during the mixing process be in the 30-35% range (Oda, 1985), and mixing time be less than 20 minutes. Insufficient mixing moisture will lead to the following problems:

(1) Moisture will not be distributed evenly among all the particles of flour, and therefore the moisture content of the sheeted dough will be patchy.

(2) If short patent flour (especially if ash < 0.38%) is used and the flour particles are too coarse, water will be absorbed slowly and structural proteins will not soften fully. The sheeted dough will consequently lack a network structure and be more-or-less composed of piled layers of flour particles (Figure 2).

(3) Because of the large energy consumption of the mixing apparatus in large-scale production, heat will be produced during mixing. The temperature of the resulting dough will rise with the dough becoming softer and stickier, making it no longer suited for the dough sheeting machines. To avoid this situation it is necessary to reduce moisture to compensate for the softening effect of higher temperature. However less mixing moisture will make the internal structure of the noodle more fragile, which leads to packaging difficulties and greater losses during transportation. In addition, in the case of steamed noodles, the use of less mixing moisture

Table 1. Types of Modern Processed Noodle Products and Their Characteristics

Item	Chilled noodle	Frozen noodle	LL noodle	Instant noodle
Definition	Raw or cooked noodles are chilled using cold water, noodles are kept refrigerated during distribution and storage.	Raw noodles are cooked, chilled in cold water, and quick-frozen.	Raw noodles are cooked, packaged, and subjected to thermal processing (a seasoning packet is included in the finished product).	Steamed noodles are dehydrated by means of deep frying or other techniques. A seasoning packet is included in the finished product.
Method of preparation	Eaten cold or warm with seasonings.	Cooked for 30 seconds to one minute in boiling water.	Noodles are steeped in boiling water or used in simple dishes.	Noodles are steeped in hot water or used in simple dishes.
Distribution and storage conditions	5-10°C	-25°C	ambient temperature	ambient temperature
Maximum length of storage	3-4 days	90-180 days	100-180 days	180 days
Product characteristics	Although noodles are very delicious on the day of manufacture, they retrograde rapidly. Restaurant and household markets are both large.	Product quality is best after defrosting in boiling water. Frozen noodles have a large food service market, particularly restaurants.	Texture is inferior to that of frozen noodles. Although storage time is relatively long, the noodles may deteriorate during the distribution process.	Texture is inferior to that of frozen noodles. Noodles lack elasticity. Easy and convenient to eat. Least likely to deteriorate during distribution.
Future prospects	Factory sanitation must be stringently controlled. Noodles made on an economic scale have room for market growth. Noodles should be packaged as complete meals together with meat and vegetable.	Countries with well-developed restaurant industries will have a large demand. A steamer may be used instead of boiling water for defrosting, after which the noodles may be added to soup.	Further development will be possible only by greatly reducing the deterioration that occurs during distribution. Packaging materials are relatively costly. Domestic makers mostly rely on foreign technology.	This type of noodle is still extremely popular in developing countries. Formulations and seasonings are different in different regions. Nonfried instant noodles have marketing appeal in developed countries.

41

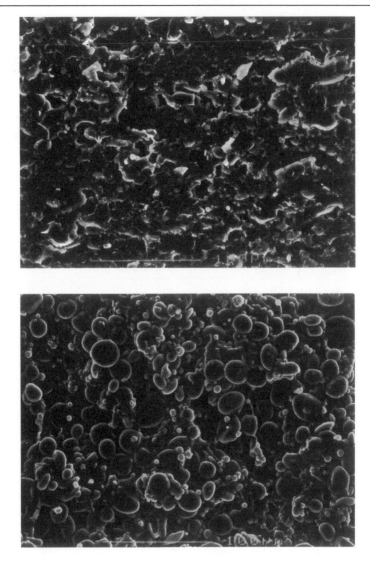

Figure 2. Microscopic structure of raw noodle.
(Top: Transverse section; Bottom: Cut surface)

usually also results in insufficient starch gelatinisation and poor noodle quality.

(4) The effect of dough aging is reduced when mixing moisture is insufficient because of the impact of inadequate water on inter-molecular mobility of the dough.

As a result of the above problems, the Japanese adopted the noodle-making technique of vacuum mixing with greater addition of moisture (Nakai, 1988). The goal of this approach was to eliminate these problems and produce noodles with higher quality. Vacuum mixing will deliver the expected results only in conjunction with correct mixing moisture. The relationship showing the most suitable mixing moisture throughout the dough mixing stage was developed by Daniels (1975). When mixing moisture was less than 38%, the required mixing energy would rise in proportion to the amount of moisture, indicating that the force between the gluten molecules was growing as the moisture increased, peaking when there was 36-40% moisture. However, the mixing energy decreased sharply when the dough moisture exceeded 40%, which implies that the dough had softened. Therefore mixing moisture in the 36-40% range is most appropriate. If it is desired to maintain constant sheeted dough hardness in the vacuum mixing process, then the appropriate mixing moisture level is in the 40-46% range (Figure 3).

Vacuum mixing with extra mixing moisture results in the following advantages:

(1) In the case of deep-fried instant noodles, the noodles will have a more satisfying texture after they have been steeped in hot water by the consumer. The interior of the fried instant noodles consists of a porous structure (caused by the frying process), and the matrix is discontinuous (due to the fact that gluten has not been fully developed). Therefore fried instant noodles lack the "chewy" consistency of most freshly-made noodles. This is due to the following reasons:

   (a) The gluten in instant noodles has not formed a network structure.

   (b) When little water is added during the mixing process, starch will not fully gelatinise during steaming. Therefore starch will not swell sufficiently when the noodles are steeped in hot water.

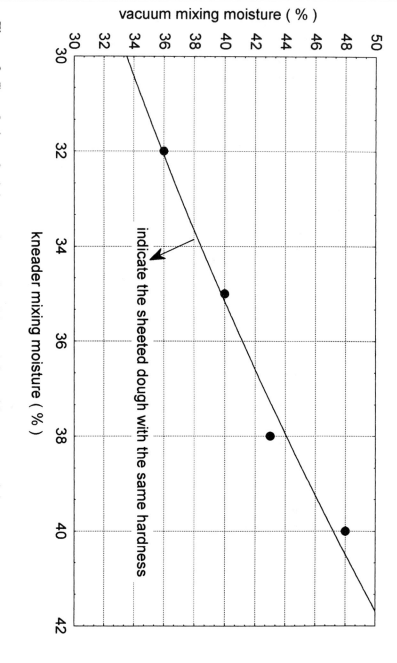

vacuum mixing moisture (%)

kneader mixing moisture (%)

indicate the sheeted dough with the same hardness

Figure 3. Correlation of mixing moisture of ambient mixing with vacuum mixing.

When extra water is added during the vacuum mixing process, starch in the noodles will gelatinise and swell to a greater extent when the noodles are being steamed, and the quality of the finished product after steeping will be superior. Moreover, if a well-developed network structure is present, the noodles will not become too mushy even if they are steeped for too long a time.

(2) As far as the dry steamed noodle is concerned, addition of extra water during the mixing process will enable full gelatinisation during steaming, which will shorten the cooking time of the finished noodles. Shortening the cooking time helps create an optimal moisture gradient in the noodles, improves their texture, and lessens the amount of noodle material that leaches out in the broth. A fully-developed gluten structure gives the noodles a continuous internal structure and makes them look more lustrous after cooking. Thanks to their stronger internal structure, the noodles will suffer less damage from mechanical impacts between the drying and packaging stages, reducing wastage. (Nakazawa, 1985; Ishibashi, 1985)

(3) In the case of chilled and refrigerated noodles, vacuum mixing with extra water can reduce the amount of time needed to cook the raw noodles and lessen the amount of leached material after rehydration. This results in the following benefits:

(a) Less water will be needed and less waste water produced.

(b) Less energy will be needed.

(c) The interior of the noodles will have a distinct moisture gradient, giving them a chewy texture.

(d) Reducing the amount of material leached from the surface of the noodles will enable better results during the back-end washing and cooling operations. The noodles will have less tendency to stick together.

(e) Because the starch swells fully (Toyoshima, 1988), the starch in the chilled noodles will have a slower retrogradation rate during refrigerated distribution.

(f) Their fully-developed gluten structure will give the noodles greater resistance to mechanical impacts during the refrigerated and frozen distribution process.

(4) Because they must receive thermal processing, the less heating Long Life noodles undergo prior to thermal processing the better. In addition, because thermal processing tends to reduce the moisture gradient between the surface and interior of the noodles, it is therefore necessary to increase the moisture gradient before thermal processing. Adding extra water during vacuum mixing can partially achieve this goal.

2.   Compound Sheeting:

In recent years Japanese food processing and machinery firms have investigated the shortcomings of machine-made noodles and the strengths of traditional hand-made noodles. The research has resulted in revolutionary breakthroughs in noodle-making machine design. Apart from using vacuum mixers with extra water, the greatest breakthrough has been the use of waved rollers in multi-roller sheeting in order to simulate the motions of noodle-making by hand (Figure 4). The network structure of gluten resulting from this process approximates that of hand-made noodles, greatly raising the quality of noodle products. The front-end manufacture of Long Life noodles in Taiwan utilises vacuum mixing in conjunction with waved rollers. In Japan many chilled and frozen noodle manufacturers also use vacuum mixing together with waved rollers in their front-end process in order to greatly improve product quality.

As the flow chart in Figure 1 shows, the differences between most types of modern processed noodles lie principally in the back-end processing. The next section will contain a detailed introduction to instant noodles, and the method of processing dry steamed noodles, chilled noodles, frozen noodles, and Long Life noodles will be described as follows:

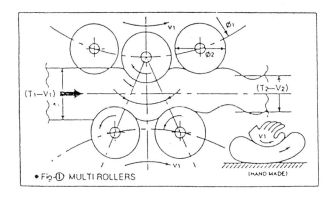

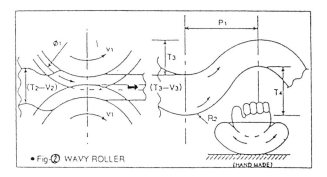

Figure 4. Multi- and waved rollers showing the sheeting mechanism of compound-sheeted dough (adopted from Yutaka, Japan).

Dry steamed noodles

Figure 5 shows some dry steamed noodle products. These products are made by steaming raw noodles and then drying them using hot air. They are eaten after being cooked in boiling water for five minutes. Although dry steamed noodles are very popular in Taiwan, customers have stated that they would like to see improvements in the following areas:

(1) Cooking time is too long and should be shortened to three minutes or less.

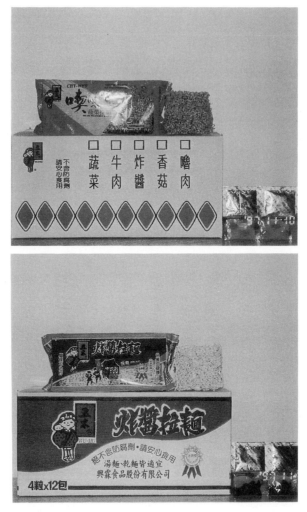

Figure 5. Dried stem-cooked noodle products (adopted from Shi-Lin Noodle Enterprise, Taiwan).

(2) Colours are not bright enough.

(3) The noodles may have a slightly rancid taste if stored for too long a time.

Processing methods that may be employed to shrink the noodles' cooking time include the following:

(1) Adopting vacuum mixing and raising the noodles' moisture content at the time of steaming in order to promote more gelatinisation during steaming.

(2) Utilising high-temperature drying (or multi-stage drying) to increase the size of pores in the noodles to allow water to penetrate the noodles more deeply at the beginning of the cooking process.

(3) Adding a starch that has a relatively low gelatinisation temperature and strong swelling capability, including natural (such as potato starch) or modified starches.

(4) Using flour with smaller particle size and lower ash content to make the noodle dough (Figure 6).

Changing flour specifications and the mixing moisture may help improve the noodles' colour and tendency to go rancid. For instance, the authors have created a special flour in which the ash content has been reduced from 0.42% to 0.39% and the flour particles are relatively fine. This flour allows the addition of 2% more mixing moisture and resolves the problems of colour and rancidity. It also shortens cooking time by roughly 20%.

Chilled and Frozen Noodles

Chilled and frozen noodles have very similar manufacturing processes. Chilled noodles are produced by boiling raw noodles and then chilling them in cold water. Frozen noodles are produced using the IQF freezing process instead of chilling (Figure 7). Chilled noodles are kept refrigerated while being distributed and in retail outlets. Frozen noodles are kept frozen during distribution and in retail outlets. Annual output of chilled noodles in Japan has reached ¥400 billion (including raw chilled noodles), and annual output of frozen noodles is ¥70 billion. Most of these noodles are sold to restaurants. Although chilled and frozen noodles are also very popular in Taiwan, most are still supplied to traditional markets. A movement is

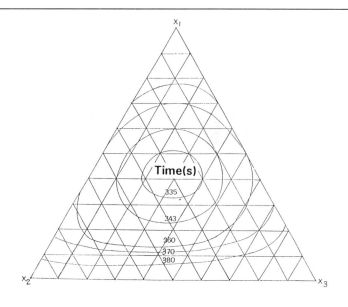

Flour	Specification		
	particle size (um)	protein (%)	ash (%)
fine(X₁)	44.15	11.30	0.43
medium(X₂)	75.77	12.60	0.35
large(X₃)	114.70	11.04	0.36

Figure 6. Effect of particle size specifications of flours on cook time for dried steam-cooked noodles.

currently under way to sell more at supermarkets and convenience stores. Thanks to the rise of the eating-out industry, chain restaurants are using even more frozen noodles. The most important feature of the frozen noodle-making process is that the noodles are cooked until they are at their tastiest and then cooled and quick-frozen (Figure 8). The noodles are then stored in a frozen condition. It is only necessary to defrost the noodles in boiling water for 20 seconds to one minute to restore them to their "tastiest" state. Being in the "tastiest" state means that the center of the noodle has good elasticity and their surface has a soft, smooth texture (Anon. 1990). This

Characteristics: 1. Prossessing a taste like just being cooked.
2. Easy to cook, only in 1 minute, if with a defroster.
3. A long time preservation is possible.

Figure 7. Frozen noodle products (adopted from T.O.M. Japan).

implies that the surface of the noodles has swelled fully, while the core maintains an appropriate level of gelatinisation. As far as moisture distribution is concerned, a steep moisture gradient is present from the outside in (Figure 9). In general, the surface has absorbed 80% water while the core has absorbed only 50%. (Hagi et al, 1995)

The quality of chilled or frozen noodles is connected with flour specifications, mixing moisture, whether or not the sheeted dough has been aged, cooking time, chilling temperature, and the noodle dimensions. Figure 10 shows the effect of flour protein content, aging time, cooking time, and chilling temperature on the noodles' tensile strength after cooking. (Cheng et al, 1997)

Figure 8. Commercial cooking and cooling equipment for chilled and frozen noodles (adopted from T.O.M.)

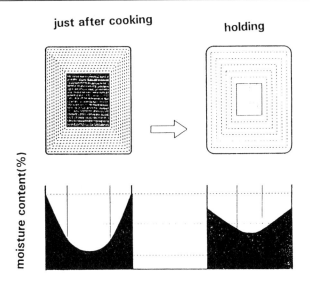

distribution of moisture across cross section

Figure 9. Changes in moisture gradient in a noodle (From Food and Science, Japan).

Long Life Noodles

Long Life (LL) noodles (Figure 11) can be sub-divided into acidified (pH≤ 4.5) and non-acidified (pH>4.5) categories. Both types must be subjected to thermal processing. In the case of acidified noodles, thermal processing takes place at a relatively low temperature of 98-100. Most national foodstuff ordinances consider non-acidified LL noodles to be canned goods that must be subjected to high temperature thermal processing.

Most currently commercialised LL noodles belong to the acidified category. The general manufacturing steps for this type of noodle include boiling, cooling, acidifying, packaging, low-temperature thermal processing, and cooling.

Key technological aspects of this process include:

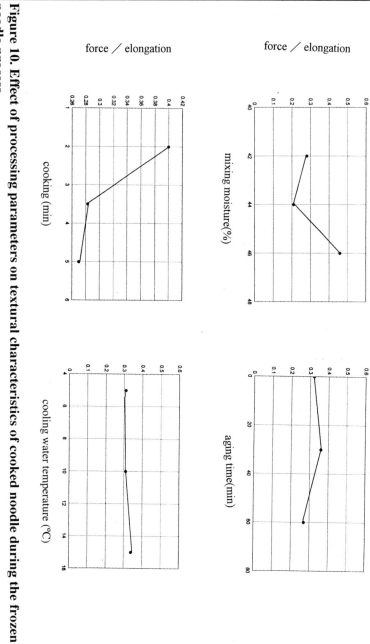

Figure 10. Effect of processing parameters on textural characteristics of cooked noodle during the frozen noodle process.

(1) The moisture content and moisture gradient of the noodles prior to thermal processing.

(2) The type of acid, concentration, and soaking time.

(3) How to maintain texture, quality, and moisture gradient during the distribution and sales stage.

(4) How to keep the noodles from sticking to each other after thermal processing.

Figure 11. Long Life noodle products (adopted from T.O.M.).

(1) The moisture content and moisture gradient of the noodles prior to thermal processing

The more time goes by cooking or steaming, the more the noodles will tend towards excessive gelatinisation and the more the moisture content of the centre of the noodles will approach that of the surface (in other words, the moisture gradient will disappear). Since LL noodles must both be cooked and subjected to thermal processing, quality will suffer if too much water is absorbed during the cooking stage. In general, moisture content prior to thermal processing should be in the range of 55-65%. Methods for controlling the moisture content and moisture gradient are as follows:

(a) Reducing cooking time (including adding extra water plus vacuum mixing, and adding modified starch).

(b) One method of preventing water from entering the center of the noodles during acid soaking is to add starch that swells readily in order to give the noodles a tighter surface structure after cooking. Another approach is to add pre-gelatinised starch and only steam the noodles in order to create a surface film. This film reduces the distance that the acid liquor can soak into the noodles and indirectly controls excessive swelling of starch in the interior of the noodles during thermal processing.

(2) The type of acid, concentration, and soaking time

Table 2. Final pH and Characteristics of Long Life noodles soaked with various acid solutions prior to thermal processing.

		Citric acid	Malic acid	Lactic acid	Gluconic acid	Acetic acid
3% organic acid solution	pH	1.94	2.02	2.03	2.30	2.49
	Colour	colourless	colourless	colourless	brown	colourless
Noodle (Cook time, 3min, soak time 1 min @ room temp.	pH	4.13	3.72	3.88	4.81	4.25
	Flavour	slightly acidic	slightly acidic	not acidic	not acidic	strongly acidic
	Taste Acceptance	acidic all right	acidic bad	acidic all right	not acidic good	acidic bad

The type and concentration of acid used in the soaking liquor will have a very significant effect on the acid taste of the final noodles. Table 2 shows the final pH and strength of acidity of the noodles after soaking in various types of acid liquors at 3% concentration. Although lactic and gluconic acid impart a relatively mild acidic taste, because gluconic acid has a high pH, the two should be ideally mixed in appropriate proportions.

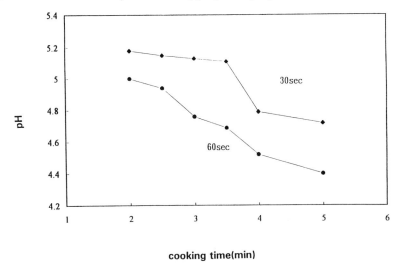

cooking time(min)

Figure 12. Effects of cooking and acid-soaking time on the final pH of Long Life noodles.

Figure 12 shows the effect of cooking time and soaking time on the pH of the noodles (noodle thickness: 1.5 mm). The 30-second soaking time curve reveals that the surface starch on noodles cooked for more than three minutes has already ruptured. Table 3 shows the combined effect of cooking time, acid concentration, and soaking time.

(3) How to maintain texture, quality and moisture gradient during the distribution and sales stage

LL noodles generally have a shelf life of three months, but the actual shelf life depends on the level of technology used by the manufacturer. The chief reason for the deterioration of quality is the gradual disappearance of moisture gradient during the distribution and sales period. This phenomenon is partially the fault of starch retrogradation. Its result is the loss of elasticity

Table 3. Final pH and moisture content of Long Life noodles subjected to various cooking and soaking times prior to thermal processing.

Cook time (min)	Lactic acid conc. (%)	Acid soak time (sec)	Moisture content (%)	pH
1.0	1.5	30	61.0	3.96
1.0	2.0	30	61.8	3.70
1.5	1.0	30	63.7	4.28
1.5	1.5	30	63.6	3.86
1.5	2.0	30	63.2	3.69

and increasing fragility (the noodles lose their tensile strength). Corrective methods include:

(a) Promoting a fully-developed network structure within the noodles.

(b) Adding egg white powder or whey protein.

(c) Adding enzymes (such as transglutaminase) during the dough mixing process to promote gluten attachment (Sakamoto et al, 1996).

(d) Controlling moisture content and moisture gradient in the noodles prior to thermal processing (already described.)

(e) Using three-layer noodle making technology to produce noodles with a different protein content on their surface and in their interior.

(f) Taking advantage of rapid swelling of the noodles' surface starch during final heating for consumption (adding pre-gelatinised starch to restore moisture gradient).

(4) How to keep the noodles from sticking to each other after thermal processing

The thermal processing of LL noodles that occurs during their manufacturing process tends to erode starch from the surface of the noodles. This may lead to stickiness after cooling and cause the packaged noodles to stick to each other. Since sticky noodles will not readily separate when they are reheated, they will have less value. Corrective methods include:

(a) Keeping the water content of the noodles in the appropriate range prior to thermal processing and preventing surface starch from swelling excessively (besides controlling processing conditions, another effective method is to spray on emulsifier prior to cooking).

(b) Making wave-shaped noodles to reduce area in contact with packaging material.

(c) Maintaining a suitable amount of empty space inside the packaging (ideally 25-35%).

(d) Treating the surface of the cooked noodles with α-amylase.

(e) Adding heat-gelation proteins such as whey protein and hydrophilic emulsifiers such as sugar ester during mixing.

Non-fried Instant Noodles

It can be said that deep fried instant noodles are the type of instant noodle that is made in the largest quantities and is most prevalent among consumers. Annual deep fried instant noodle output is roughly ¥480 billion in Japan and NT$10 billion in Taiwan. This type of noodle is also becoming increasingly popular in mainland China. The chief reason for the popularity of deep fried instant noodles is their ease of rehydration and excellent flavour.

But because of consumers' greater acceptance of health foods in recent years, oily foods are gradually losing favour in the developed nations, and non-fried instant noodles are emerging on the scene. In terms of quality, these noodles are not in the least inferior to fried instant noodles, and may even by superior. Japan currently has the most experience with

59

commercialised non-fried instant noodle products, and has achieved the best product quality. Japanese makers include Toyosuisan, Myojo Foods, and Kanebo, etc. Although similar products are found in other countries, they must be cooked in boiling water (and therefore cannot be considered instant noodles; when steeped in hot water, these noodles either have too slow a rehydration rate or lose their chewy texture and are perceived unfavourably by consumers). Last year research at the authors Institute successfully developed a non-fried instant noodle under commission from a major Taiwanese noodle firm, and we believe that non-fried instant noodles will soon be marketed in Taiwan.

Differences in the Structure of Deep Fried and Non-fried Instant Noodles

The basic requirement made of instant noodles is of convenience. This is to say that they should be able to rehydrate after being steeped in hot water for a very short time (less than 3-4 minutes). As far as fried instant noodles are concerned, their front-end manufacturing process is identical with that for fresh or dried noodles (Kuwahara, 1987), the only difference is that the former type of noodles are fried in high-temperature oil. This frying causes flash expansion of the noodles' moisture and results in a porous spongy structure created by steam (Figure 13). However, since the starch has not swelled fully, texture after rehydration is inferior to that of boiled fresh or dried noodles. Complete swelling of starch is the reason that fried instant noodles have a good texture when cooked in boiling water. Non-fried instant noodles can basically be divided among two types: the non-expanded type and the expanded type. There are significant structural differences between these two types (Figure 14). The former is rather thin and has a tight structure while the latter is thicker and has a porous, honeycomb-like structure. The former is dehydrated after expansion, while the latter uses high-temperature expansion to produce a porous structure and insure that water will be able to quickly enter and rehydrate the noodles. The greatest difference between non-fried and fried instant noodles is that the former is dehydrated by some means other than frying. Moreover, a technique other than frying is used to expand non-fried instant noodles and produce a porous structure.

Figure 13. Microscopic structure of fried instant noodle.

The general manufacturing process for non-fried instant noodles is shown in Figure 1. However, one cannot see the differences from ordinary dry steamed noodles (this type of product is very popular in Taiwan where the noodles are cooked in boiling water before they are eaten, and the cooking time is shorter than in the case of dried noodles) from the flow chart alone. In addition, the flow chart does not show differences in the manufacture of expanded and non-expanded noodles. Technological differences in the manufacture of expanded and non-expanded noodles are described as follows:

Non-Expanded Type

To achieve a short steeping time, non-expanded products are generally either relatively thin or have fully gelatinised starch. Furthermore, because the starch will be restored to a fully swelled condition after rehydration, and the noodles will have a well-developed gluten network structure, they will exhibit a good chewy texture. Therefore it is necessary to use vacuum mixing and the addition of extra water (>38%) to produce these noodles. The reasons for this are as follows:

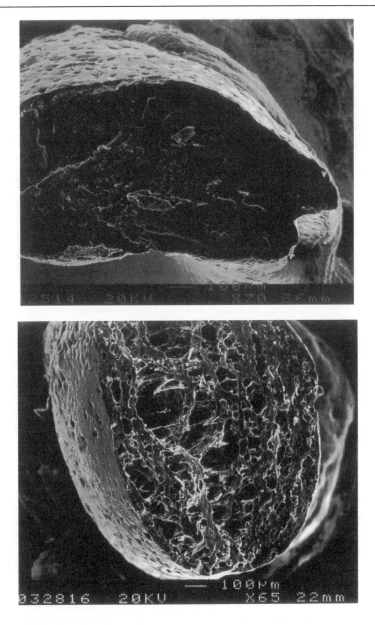

Figure 14. Microscopic structure of non-expanded (Top) and expanded (Bottom) nonfried instant noodle.

(1) The noodles will have a fully-developed gluten network structure only if mixing moisture is sufficient.

(2) The noodles will have enough water for starch gelatinisation during steaming only if mixing moisture is sufficient.

(3) Sufficient mixing moisture will insure an even moisture distribution among the flour particles during mixing. This will result in dough with a homogeneous internal structure.

(4) Vacuum mixing can insure that moisture fully enters the flour particles within a very short time. Therefore noodles produced with extra water during the mixing stage are suitable for mechanical processing (suitable for roller sheeting).

Therefore vacuum mixing is necessary to insure the chewy texture of the products after rehydration. Because non-expanded noodles are rather thin, they are mostly considered Chinese (alkaline) noodles, and must contain a suitable amount of alkali. Because their alkali content must conform to the drying temperature (otherwise they will tend to have brownish spots), this type of product generally has a drying temperature of less than $90^{\circ}C$ and typically in the $60\text{-}80^{\circ}C$ range. To achieve fast rehydration and a good texture, 10-20% starch is usually added. Because the addition of starch will reduce protein content, the specifications of these noodles must include:

(1) Low starch damage.

(2) Particle diameter must be small (70) to insure that moisture is evenly distributed.

(3) Protein content must be 11% or more.

(4) Ash must be 0.4% or less.

In general, mixing moisture during vacuum mixing should be in the 38 - 42% range. If the water content is calculated, it should be in the 37.7 - 40% range. It is difficult to obtain optimal results from vacuum mixing when mixing moisture is less than 36%. On the other hand, the dough will tend to form large lumps if the mixing moisture is too high (>46%), and these lumps will cause difficulties during mechanical processing.

The most common quality defects seen non-expanded products include (1) slow rehydration rate, (2) sticking among the individual noodles, and (3) poor texture after rehydration (in general, use of non-expanded noodles is limited to thin Chinese noodle product. A poor texture is usually due to incomplete swelling of starch and lack of gluten firmness). Apart from whether or not natural or modified starch has been added to achieve a faster rehydration rate, the degree of starch gelatinisation during after steaming can affect the texture of the rehydrated noodles. Generally speaking, steaming is carried out under a pressure of 0.5 kg/cm^2 - 1.5 kg/cm^2 and a temperature of 98°C for approximately 2-3 minutes, depending on the noodles' thickness and moisture content. When vacuum mixing is not employed, mixing moisture is relatively low and water is usually sprayed on the surface of the noodles before steaming. This sprayed water promotes starch gelatinisation during steaming. Otherwise boiling water may be sprayed on the noodles after steaming to promote starch gelatinisation and improve transparency. In addition, the chief factors affecting the rehydration rate are the porosity of the noodle cake (the transverse layering after steaming is similar to that of structure of the upper and lower layers of ordinary bag-packaged instant noodles) and the spraying of emulsifier on the surface of the noodles before and during steaming. The noodle cake of bag-packaged instant noodles ordinarily has a rather high porosity. Besides reducing sticking between the individual pieces of noodle, the spraying of emulsifier can reduce the surface tension of the water during steeping and allow quicker entry of moisture.

Whether or not the gluten has achieved a full network structure and whether or not the gluten molecules have formed a permanent linkage during steaming (Kojima et al, 1995) will have a decisive influence on the firmness of the noodles after rehydration. Besides controlling the protein quality of the flour, adding CaCO$_3$ can also strengthen the gluten structure. In the manufacturing process, dough aging and the rotational speed of the rollers have the greatest effect on finished product quality. The specific effects of these steps are discussed as follows:

Dough Aging

There are four goals of aging: (Kogawa, 1984; Ito, 1988)

(1) To cause moisture to be more evenly distributed.

(2) To promote the formation of disulfide bonds.

(3) To encourage gluten relaxation prior to sheeting.

(4) To form bonds between gluten and oils (especially phospholipids), increasing the mutual reactivity of gluten.

As far as the former two goals are concerned, vacuum mixing with the addition of extra water can achieve identical results. The reason for this is that the dough produced in vacuum mixing systems can usually be sheeted immediately after compounding without any aging. However, in all cases whether or not aging has been performed will have a significant effect on steaming, even when sufficient water is added during mixing. As Figure 15 shows, whether or not the sheeted dough has been aged has a very significant effect on the degree of starch gelatinisation during steaming. A high degree of gelatinisation occurs in dough that has been aged, and a low degree of gelatinisation occurs in dough that has not. The reason for this may be, (1) because the gluten will not soften if the dough has not been aged it will solidify during steaming and suppress starch swelling, or (2) moisture has become more evenly distributed and partial, premature gelatinisation of starch does not occur and hence blocks the entry of water. As Figure 15 indicates, the aging of sheeted dough makes ΔH value of starch gelatinisation become larger, while the ΔH value of exothermic reaction becomes smaller. This shows that new protein bonds might form during the aging period and moisture achieves a more even distribution. Therefore lessening the mechanical energy imparted to the sheeted dough during rolling should have a positive effect on the structure of the rehydrated finished product. Therefore slowing the rotational speed of sheeting and rolling, while allowing the dough to pass through the rollers for a longer period of time, should promote better gelatinisation during steaming (better

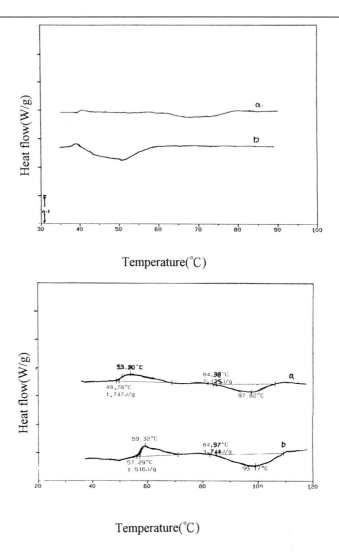

Figure 15. Effect of compounded dough aging on thermoproperties of raw and cooked noodle (Top: Cooked noodles; Bottom: Raw noodles, a: non-aged, b: aged).

heat penetration). Furthermore, slightly lengthening the duration of sheeting and rolling will also have the following advantages:

(1) The gluten will have a better network structure: Because typical sheeting speed subjects the dough to repeated large deformations within a very short time (ie. the deformation rate is large), the gluten structure is easily damaged. Therefore decreasing the deformation rate will help maintain a more intact gluten structure.

(2) Further sheeting of the dough after aging can press out gas and increase the density of the noodles.

(3) Reducing the hardness of the sheeting surface: Due to the velocity distribution during sheeting, the faster the velocity, the easier it is to shear gluten underneath the surface of the dough.

(4) Aging of the sheeted dough results in more smooth surfaces (including raw and cooked noodles). This can reduce the noodles' tendency to stick to each other.

Cutting and Steaming

After being sheeted, the dough must be cut to the proper length. Beneath the cutting bar is a bumper that squeezes the noodles into a wave shape before steaming. Besides causing the starch to gelatinise, steaming also must allow the full swelling that is needed for a fast rehydration rate and a pleasing texture after steeping. Apart from full gelatinisation of the starch, the gluten must assume a fixed, permanent structure during steaming. In order to prevent damage from excessive swelling or compression of the gluten structure from too rapid swelling, the gluten's permanent structure should take shape before the starch completes swelling. Therefore the difference between the starch gelatinisation temperature and the gluten's denaturation temperature is very important. Both processes compete for water. As Figure 15 shows, starch gelatinisation does not begin until a temperature of greater than $80°C$ is reached, even when abundant water is present >70%. Therefore the core of the noodles must reach a temperature of at least $80°C$ during steaming. The noodles will only have an approximately 41% moisture content even if 44% mixing moisture is used, and the gelatinisation temperature will therefore be even higher. Thus it seems to be a difficult matter to get the wheat starch in the noodles to gelatinise fully during the steaming stage. To insure that the finished product has a satisfactory texture and a fast rehydration rate, promoting the full gelatinisation of starch during steaming is an indispensable task. Apart from the methods already mentioned, making pits in the surface of the noodles so that water can enter the noodles more quickly during rehydration is also effective (Figure 16).

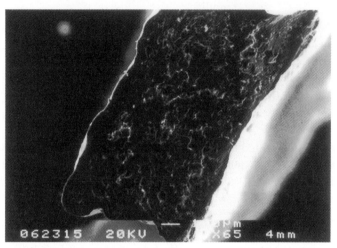

Figure 16. Microscopic view of air cells in nonfried instant noodle (nonexpanded type).

Chilling and Drying

When deep fried instant noodles are being made, the frying step serves to dehydrate the noodles. Deep frying is basically a type of drying. In addition, because the surfaces of the fried noodles absorb oil, the noodles in the noodle cake will not stick to each other. Even if it appears that the noodles are packed closely together, steeping in hot water will cause them to separate. However, this is not the case for non-fried instant noodles. The most thorny technical problem with regard to non-fried instant noodles is how to prevent the noodles from sticking to each other during drying. This includes the problem of sticking when wave-shaped noodles are stacked in layers, resulting in uneven drying. During the distribution process where the noodles are attached to each other they will retrograde, so that the noodles rehydrate unevenly and have a poor texture. In severe cases the noodles will not separate even when steeped in hot water. Some manufacturers have attempted to solve this problem by spraying oil on the surface of the noodles after steaming, but this has the drawback of inhibiting the evaporation of water during drying and necessitating a longer drying time. Other approaches to solving this problem have included both changing the manufacturing process and modifying the dough formulation:

(1) Using rounder noodles to minimise the area of contact.

(2) Adding an emulsifier or a small amount of starch with high amylose content (such as mung bean starch). The gel-forming nature and ability to form a film of these substances prevents mutual adhesion between the noodles.

(3) Two-stage steaming method: This method consists of steaming, surface emulsification, and further steaming. The key part of this method is causing starch at the surface of the noodles to swell to a certain level and then applying an emulsifier to prevent the starch from swelling excessively during the second steaming stage. This will prevent interior material from coming out and causing stickiness.

(4) Cooling method: The objective of cooling the noodles after steaming is to prevent excessive starch gelatinisation (especially when the interior of the noodles has a high moisture content). Another important function of cooling is to remove excess water from the surface of the noodles using a forced cold air draft. The drop in temperature will also cause soluble starch components on the surface of the noodles to form a film more quickly.

(5) Cooling and washing method: In this method the noodles are cooled rapidly after steaming. The objective of this method is to cause the gelatinised starch particles on the surface of the noodles to harden (in general, the temperature of the noodle surface must be kept at $10°C$ or below). The objective of washing is to rinse away soluble starchy material from the surface of the noodles. But if the surface temperature is not low enough, already-swelled starch particles will continue to absorb water. Furthermore, excess water may cause starchy material at

the surface of the noodles to dissolve, with the result that the noodles will still stick together during drying.

Main technical aspects of the drying process

The drying of non-fried instant noodles includes the following aspects:

(1) Formation of the noodle cake.

(2) Drying equipment and conditions.

Methods of forming the noodle cake include (1) the irregular direction method (Figure 17) and (2) the stacking method similar to that of fried instant noodles. In the former method, the contact area between the noodles is large and space inside the noodle cake is small, but there is a high degree of flexibility in adjusting the noodle cake's weight. In contrast, in the latter method, there is a small area of contact between the noodles and space inside the noodle cake is large, which facilitates the rapid and even entry of water when the noodles are steeped. However, this method allows little flexibility in controlling the weight of individual noodle cakes (therefore the second method is less suitable when the weight requirements for individual packaged products are relatively stringent). As far as drying efficiency is concerned, the former method requires more time. To prevent uneven drying, the temperature must be relatively low. This implies a time-consuming drying process. In addition, a larger investment in drying equipment may also be required.

Figure17. Noodle cake showing compacted array of noodle strands.

Generally speaking, drying must reduce the water content of noodles to 12% or lower. Drying methods include:

(1) Hot air drying.

(2) Microwave drying.

(3) Combined microwave and hot air drying.

(4) Combined infrared and microwave drying.

(5) Humidity-adjustment drying method (also termed the high-humidity drying method).

Typically, the hot air drying method or the humidity-adjustment drying method is used to dry non-expanded non-fried instant noodles. In the hot air drying method, the temperature, air speed, and humidity will affect the quality and form of the noodles. In addition, it is important to note that the noodles will be firmer if some of their surface moisture can be evaporated away after steaming and before drying. This can insure greater empty space and less contact area within the noodle cake, which in turn will increase the drying rate and facilitate more even drying. The humidity of the drying environment is controlled during the humidity adjustment drying method. The objectives of this method are as follows:

(1) To use the humidity of the drying environment to control the mass transfer rate of the noodles during the drying process to insure that the noodles have an even moisture throughout.

(2) To give the surface of the noodles a glossy appearance.

(3) To reduce the dissolution of starchy material from the surface of the noodles during steeping.

Humidity is generally at 25-40% and temperature 94-100°C in this method. As far as objectives (2) and (3) are concerned, a possible explanation is that the starch undergoes a type of hot/humid processing while being dried, and this processing apparently strengthens the aggregation of gluten proteins, which tightens the surface structure of the noodles. Moreover, even drying prevents the noodles from cracking during the drying process and therefore lessens the dissolution of interior material to a certain extent on rehydration.

Second Generation Non-fried Instant Noodles - Expanded Non-fried Instant Noodles

Product Characteristics

It can be said that expanded non-fried instant noodles are second-generation non-fried instant noodles. The differences between expanded and non-expanded non-fried instant noodles are shown in Table 3. These differences chiefly arise from differences in the structure of these types of noodles. The chief characteristic of the structure of the expanded noodles is their porous, honeycomb-like internal structure. This structure allows the rapid entry of water and thus speeds up the rehydration rate. There are no major differences between expanded and non-expanded noodles in terms of manufacturing processes and equipment.

Essential Quality goals

The manufacturing process for expanded non-fried instant noodles must achieve the following quality goals:

(1) Rapid rehydration (3-4 minutes when steeped in water at a temperature of 85-95°C).

(2) Chewy texture is superior to that of ordinary instant noodles.

(3) Even rehydration.

Key Goals of Manufacturing Process

(1) Creation of a porous structure.

(2) Creation of a continuous matrix around the pores in the noodle (Figure 18).

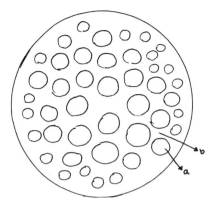

Figure 18. Ideal cell distribution in expanded type nonfried instant noodle (a: air cell, b: matrix).

(3) Solution of the problem of adhesion of individual noodles.

(4) Even drying (expansion) of the noodles.

(5) Maintaining good texture after steeping.

Porous Structure

Creating an evenly porous structure is a key technical aspect of the manufacture of non-fried instant noodles. Critical points include:

(1) How to form an evenly porous structure.

(2) How to give the noodles with such porous structures a good texture after rehydration.

There is a fundamental contradiction between point (1) and point (2). According to the principles of noodle-making, only noodles with a dense and well-developed gluten network structure will have a good chewy texture. Therefore it is necessary to achieve a compromise between points (1) and (2) before further developing pore-making technology. Figure 18 shows a model of an ideal porous structure in which the pores are separated by matrix. The pores provide hot water with avenues for entering the matrix, and also provide the matrix with space into which the starch can swell. After rehydration, starch in the matrix will swell and make the pores disappear, giving the noodles a pleasing texture. But only a continuous matrix in between the pores will insure a continuous structure of gluten proteins. This tells us that key aspects of the manufacturing process are controlling the number and size distribution of pores, and controlling the rehydration and continuity of the matrix. This is described as follows:

(1)   Controlling the number of pores

The following methods of producing pores are most commonly used:

   (a). Addition of chemical leavening.

   (b). Fermentation method.

   (c). Method of using existing gas pores in the dough. (Miki et al 1988)

No matter which method is used, the production and distribution of pores involves the following three stages: (1) the number and size of gas bubble nuclei prior to expansion; (2) the production of gas; and (3) the diffusion of gas dissolved in the matrix during expansion. In light of the authors' research and experience, the first stage occurs during mixing until before steaming, the second stage occurs during steaming and before drying, and the third stage occurs during drying, which is the main expansion stage.

(2)   Formation of gas bubble nuclei

Throughout all process stages the sheeted dough always contains minute gas bubbles, termed "gas bubble nuclei." In expansion-type instant noodles these bubbles are formed during mixing and compounding. Although there are relatively few bubbles in dough produced by the vacuum mixing process, air is entrapped in the dough during the compounding stage, and the gluten structure has a good ability to hold what bubbles there are. In addition, the sheeting process results in an ideal number and distribution of gas bubbles.

(3)   Growth and disappearance of bubbles

Gas bubble nuclei in the dough may either grow or disappear. Factors that may affect the stability of gas bubble nuclei include the size of the bubbles, the liquid surface tension, visco-elastic property of the dough, and the saturation concentration of gases (CO_2 or O_2) in the liquid. In comparison with other food systems, gas bubble nuclei are relatively stable in dough due to the gluten structure. At ambient temperature the bubbles will not shrink or expand significantly. Even if the bubbles grow or shrink due to the rise in temperature during steaming, starch gelatinisation will fix the internal structure of the noodles and prevent the bubbles from growing too large. Therefore any bubble shrinkage or growth must occur before a temperature of 80°C is reached. Furthermore, differences in the conduction of heat within the noodles, bubbles in the superficial layer of the noodles may grow or shrink quite rapidly. Some bubbles may break through the surface of the noodles and create open pores (Figure 19). This phenomenon will increase the rapidity with which hot water can enter the noodles when they are being steeped. Because starch in the centre of the noodles gelatinises relatively slowly and incompletely, flash expansion is permitted during the drying stage.

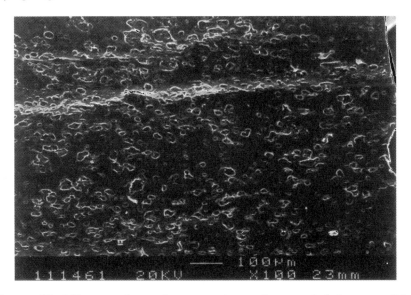

Figure 19. Microscopic surface structure of expanded type nonfried instant noodle.

The concentration of chemical leavening in the sheeted dough, whether or not it is distributed evenly, and the rate at which the chemical leavening contacts acid salt and produced gas are extremely important. The addition of chemical leavening and acid salt should be performed in stages in order to avoid large amounts of gas being produced and lost due to presence of free water which may exist during the initial phase of mixing because of incomplete absorption by the flour. For example, if the chemical leavening is added early in the mixing stage (in a water solution), while the acidic compound may be added later in the mixing stage after water has been completely absorbed by the flour.

Yano (1988) proposed that the critical radius of bubbles growing in the dough could be determined by means of equation (1):

$$r_c = 3\sigma / E \quad (1)$$

Where r_c is the critical radius, σ is the surface tension of water and E is the relaxation elasticity of the dough.

Equation (1) indicates that the growth of gas bubbles:

(a)   is connected with the water content of the dough.

(b)   is connected with the surface tension, and elasticity of the dough.

(c)   is connected with the temperature and the rate of temperature rise (because temperature will affect both σ and E).

Figure 20 shows how bubbles in the dough change when the temperature is varied (because the temperature will rise rapidly in the superficial layer of the noodles, the gelatinisation of starch will cause the structure to quickly solidify, and therefore E will become very large. This implies that bubble nuclei larger than r_c will become more numerous) (Figure 21). This, and the fact that the temperature in the interior of the noodle will rise more slowly than at the surface during steaming, explains why pores in the interior of non-fried instant noodles are large, while those near the surface are smaller.

(4)   Expansion of Bubbles:

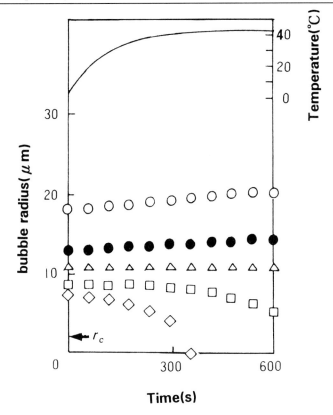

Figure 20. Bubble size change with time during temperature rise in dough (From Yano).

In general, the noodles experience no significant expansion through the steaming stage. This is shown by the fact that the transverse area of the noodles does not significantly increase after steaming. Therefore expansion is usually performed during drying. The following factors may affect the expansion mechanism and the degree of expansion:

(a) Mixing moisture and the drying temperature.

(b) The quality of the gluten structure.

(c) The drying procedures.

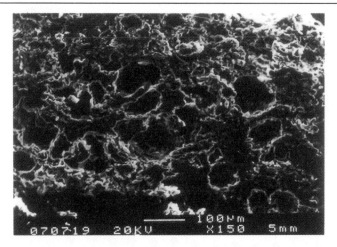

Figure 21. Microscopic internal structure of expanded type nonfried instant noodle.

(d) Surface hardness and moisture distribution.

(e) Directional stress from the cutting blade and sheeting surface.

These factors are discussed in detail as follows:

Moisture in the noodles during expansion (Wu et al, 1997)

Figure 22 shows the effect of different drying temperatures and noodle moisture contents on the expansion rate (the moisture content indicated by the abscissa coordinates is the mixing moisture). The product has not expanded when the drying temperature is $110^{\circ}C$, and below $110^{\circ}C$ the greater the product's moisture content, the greater the shrinkage. However, above $110^{\circ}C$ expansion increases with an increase in moisture content. Nevertheless, Figure 22 does not reveal the structure of the noodles after expansion. There is a tendency for the noodles to have large pores and become hollow (Figure 23) when the moisture content is high. This may be caused by large gas bubble nuclei forming inside the noodles during steaming or by aggregation of bubbles formed during expansion prior to the time the structure solidifies.

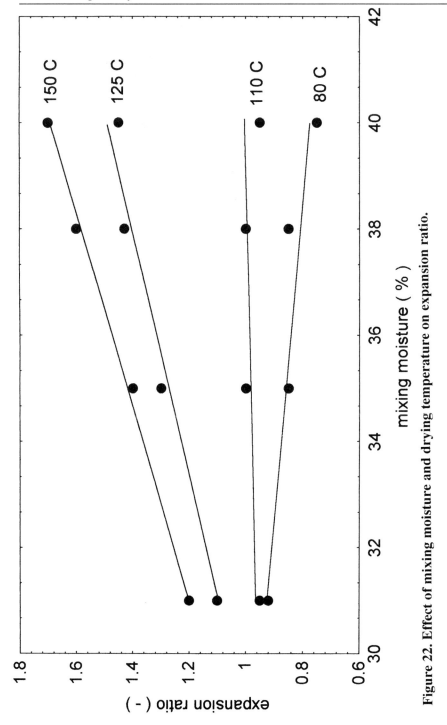

Figure 22. Effect of mixing moisture and drying temperature on expansion ratio.

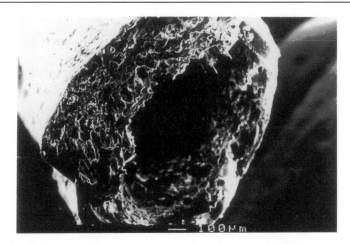

Figure 23. Large hole in expanded nonfried instant noodle.

Necessity of a gluten network structure

Because it allows the gluten network to form fully, a mixing moisture of 38-42% during the mixing stage will result in the best quality when making alkaline noodles or regular oriental noodles (not including Wulong noodles). In addition, when expansion occurs during drying, the force of the expanding bubbles may cause rupturing if the gluten does not have a good structure, which results in poor quality after steeping. Therefore the dough must have a sufficient moisture content during mixing. However, because too high a moisture content will cause expansion quality to deteriorate, it is best if the drying of the steamed noodles proceeds in stages, which involves the design of the drying procedure.

Drying procedure

The basic principle of multi-stage drying (Wu et al, 1997) is to remove part of the moisture from the noodles prior to high-temperature expansion. The theoretical basis for this procedure is as follows:

(a) After a relatively low temperature is used to remove part of the noodles' moisture content, firmness will increase due to reduced moisture content in the matrix near pores. Since the concentration of

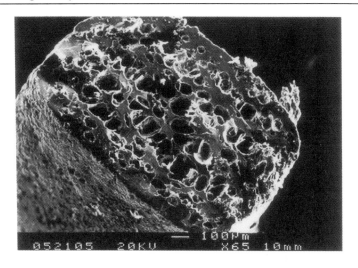

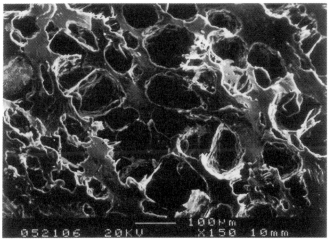

Figure 24. Microscopic internal structure showing uniform air cells as well as homogeneous matrix for expanded nonfried instant noodle using two-step drying method.

CO_2 in the water will rise, a relatively large number of bubbles can exceed the expansion energy level. This facilitates the achievement of

81

the goal of "even expansion." Thus the product will have a fine structure and good matrix continuity.

(b) Because there will be less of a temperature difference between the surface and interior of the noodles after the first stage of drying, high-temperature drying will be able to achieve the goal of "even expansion."

The temperature should ideally be 100-120°C during the first drying stage. A temperature greater than 120°C will cause expansion within a short period of time, making it difficult to control production. On the other hand, a temperature below 100°C will lead to wrinkles and deformation in the noodles. Figure 24 shows the results of initial drying at 120°C followed by high-temperature expansion at 150°C. This structure is quite similar to the ideal structure shown in Figure 18.

Differences in physical characteristics between the surface and interior of the noodles (hardness, moisture content)

In the case of expanded non-fried instant noodles, even expansion plays a key role in insuring quality. Uneven expansion will result in surface peeling and separation when the finished product is steeped.

The reason for this is the directionality of large bubbles under the surface and/or internal bubbles resulting from uneven expansion (Figure 25).

(a) Large bubbles under the surface: From mixing until cutting, the surface of the noodles will lose part of its moisture to the air (chiefly through the sheeted surface) because of the relatively low humidity of the air conditioned environment. Besides making the sheeted surface harder, this may also cause uneven stress during sheeting, which can lead to twisting of gluten under the sheeted surface and the production of large gas bubble nuclei. In addition, loss of moisture from the surface of the sheeted dough may affect starch gelatinisation during steaming and thereby cause product quality to suffer.

(b) Uneven moisture distribution is often seen in sheeted dough produced in a constant pressure mixing process. The reason for this is

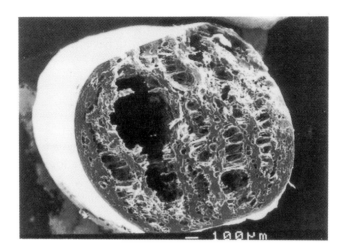

Figure 25. Expanded type nonfried instant noodle showing large air cells beneath the surface as well as significantly oriented air cells.

that the limited amount of water added during mixing is unable to evenly and fully moisten the flour particles. This may lead to a patchy distribution of gas bubble nuclei in terms of size and number, resulting in uneven expansion.

(c) Directional stress from the cutting blade and sheeting surface: The cutting and sheeting operations may both cause differential stress in the surface of the noodles. In other words, stress in the vicinity of gas bubble nuclei may have directional characteristics. This may lead to directional gas bubble nuclei and the emergence of directional form after expansion. In addition, the limited amount of water added during constant pressure mixing is insufficient to allow the gluten to develop fully. After cutting the cut ends are usually uneven and have many pores (Figure 2) that prevent the retention of gas during expansion. These phenomena tend to cause the directional expansion of bubbles. In general, because the cut surfaces have relatively poor gas retention, the gas bubbles will tend to expand in the direction of the two sheeted surfaces if uneven expansion occurs. This is the reason that the thickness expansion rate is much greater than the width expansion rate.

In accordance with the above conclusions, the following methods of insuring even expansion and even bubble growth have been proposed:

(a) Noodles' width/thickness ratio should not be too large; a ratio of 1.0-1.3 is best.

(b) In vacuum mixing, mixing moisture should be sufficient to allow the complete formation of gluten. Completely-formed gluten will leave the cutting blade smooth and clean, preventing damage to the noodles' gas retention ability.

(c) Properly controlling the rotational speed of the sheeting rollers can avoid excessive shearing force.

(d) The surfaces of the noodles may be moistened after cutting and before steaming in order to make up for water lost from sheeted surfaces.

Texture of Expanded Non-fried Instant Noodles and Influencing Factors

In the case of most fried instant noodles, expansion during frying produces an external and internal porous structure that enables a fast rehydration rate during steeping (Figure 13). However, if fried instant noodles that have been boiled for three minutes are compared with those that have been steeped in hot water for three minutes, the former will have a distinctly superior chewy texture. This tells us that starch plays an important role in determining texture. This principle also applies in the case of non-fried instant noodles. In other words, there is a direct relationship between the texture and whether the starch has swelled fully during steeping.

Although the expansion of noodles can promote a faster rehydration rate, it is still necessary to have gas present even when the interior of the noodles has a pre-existing porous structure. Therefore, if the degree of expansion is too great, the hot water will have difficulty penetrating to the centre of the noodles during steeping. This is due to the force of gas escaping from the

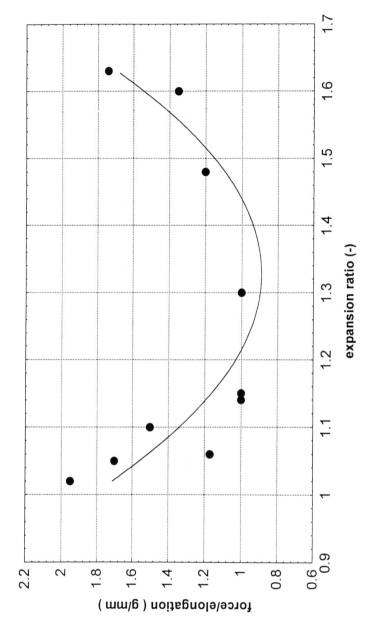

Figure 26. Correlation of force/elongation to expansion ratio for nonfried instant noodles.

centre of the noodle on heating, the swelling of starch around the surface layer of the noodle, and the temperature drop of the steeping water. Figure 26 shows the relationship between the degree of expansion and the stretch force/elongation distance in non-fried instant noodles that have been made using a two-stage drying process. The larger the degree of expansion, the larger the stretch force/elongation distance ratio will be, until the stretch force/elongation distance ratio reaches a maximum when the expansion ratio is roughly 1.4. But if the expansion ratio is greater than 1.4, the stretch force/elongation distance ratio will decrease in proportion to expansion.

The size of the pores and the number of bubbles directly influence the texture of the noodles after rehydration. Besides affecting the manner in which hot water enters the noodles, structural factors also affect the rate at which starch swells and the density of the noodles after rehydration. Although no existing literature or data reports discuss the effect of pore size, pore number, and the thickness of the intervening matrix on rehydration rate and texture after rehydration, noodle makers and researchers are all focussing their attention on achieving a suitable number of pores, a narrow pore size distribution, an even distribution of pores throughout the noodles, continuous matrix surrounding the pores, and a reasonable matrix thickness.

Directions of future technology development

The evolution of noodle processing technology has already progressed from "hand-made noodles" to "machine-made noodles" to "machine-made noodles possessing the quality of hand-made noodles". Certainly the level of processing technology is growing ever higher. Although not every modern noodle product can be considered an "instant noodle," in fact all have more or less the characteristic of "instant-ness." If manufacturing, quality changes during distribution, and quality when eaten are taken into consideration, then frozen noodles most closely approximate the quality of traditional hand-made noodles. The others cannot match the quality of hand-made noodles. Therefore future technology development will include the following:

1.   Deep fried instant noodles

Efforts will include reducing the amount of absorbed oil and improving the texture of the noodles without slowing their rehydration rate. Structural changes will be made in manufacturing systems (such as adopting vacuum mixing and increasing added water to facilitate the appearance of a gluten structure, performing deep frying after steaming and initial drying, or adopting separate low- and high-temperature deep frying stages).

2.   Dry steamed noodles

Progress will be made towards the goal of short cooking time (less than three minutes). Feasible methods include the formulation of "quick-cooking specialty flour", the use of other drying techniques (such as microwaves or superheated steam), or the use of expansion to create pores in the noodles, etc.

3.   Chilled and frozen noodles

Equipment modifications that reduce the amount of water used during and chilling will be studied. As far as process technology is concerned, feasible methods include shortening cooking time and reducing dissolution of surface material. Efforts will be made to find ways of reducing retrogradation of chilled noodles during the distribution process. In the case of frozen noodles, work will be done to help the food service industry to use steaming to defrost noodles, so that customers can consume the product immediately they enter the shop with hot soup being added directly to the pre-defrosted noodle.

4.   Long Life noodles

Future development work will focus on high-temperature thermal processing (because many people don't like the acid taste of acidified noodles). However, a major challenge is how to maintain quality throughout the distribution stage for noodles that have undergone high-temperature thermal processing.

All of the above efforts will be closely connected with how deep hot water penetrates into the noodles during the initial phase of cooking or steeping (the first 30 seconds to one minute), physical-chemical structural transformations of starch and gluten during this period, and the rate of these transformations. In other words, "unravelling the mystery of the noodle cooking mechanism" may serve as the basis for improving processing technology or making structural breakthroughs in processing systems.

References

Cheng, M.C. and Wu, T.P. (1997). Improvement of acidified long-life noodle P64-86 in "Technical Report of Technical Improvement for Grain based foods" Industry Bureau, ed. Taipei.

Daniels, N.W.R. (1975). Some effects of water in wheat flour doughs in "Water Relations of Foods" page 573-586. R.D. Duskworth., ed. Academic press INC (London) LTD.

Hagi, T., Kawai, T. and Ozeki, I. (1995). The improvement of noodle quality stabilization Food and Science (Japan) Vol. 37:1-9.

Ishibashi, S. (1985). Dry noodles process using dough mixed up with high moisture. Food and Science (Japan) Vol. 4:102.

Ito, M. (1988). Flour materials for noodles processing using dough mixed up with high moisture. Food and Science Vol. (Extra):31-34.

Kogawa, G. (1984). Noodle aging in "Food aging" p333-347. Shin sato ed. Kohrin, Tokyo.

Kuwahara, M. (1987). Basic processing technology of non-fried instant chinese noodles. Food and Science Vol (Extra):65-66.

Kuwahara, M. (1987). Basic processing technology of deep fried instant chinese noodles. Food and Science Vol (Extra):66-71.

Kojima, M., Togawa, T., Murase, M., Totani, S., and Sugimoto, M. (1995). Effects of addition of water and sodium chloride on microstructure and rheological properties of noodle. Nippon Shokuhin Kagaku Kogaku Kaishi Vol 42(11):899-906.

Miki, E., Yoshida, M., and Yamano, Y. (1988). Change in density of dough during Japanese noodle making. Nippon Shokuhin Kogyo Gakkaishi Vol.35(11):735-741.

Nakazawa, S. (1985). Vacuum mixer and noodle processing technology. Food and Science (Japan) Vol.(Extra)120-122.

Nakai, M. (1988). The utilisation of vacuum mixing in noodle processing. Food and Science (Japan) Vol.8:107-111.

Oda, M. (1985). Manufacture of aged noodles with high mixing moisture. Food and Science. (Japan) Vol.(Extra):21-23.

On everything of Frozen Noodles. Anon. (1990). Journalist Agency of Food Journalism. Tokyo.

Sakamoto, H., Yamazaki, K., Kaga, C., Yamamoto, Y., Ito, R., and Kurosawa, Y. (1996). Strength enhancement by addition of microbial transglutaminase during chinese noodles processing. Nippon Shokuhin Kagaku Kogaku Kaishi Vol.43(5):598-602.

Toyoshima, R.G. (1988). Starch gelatinisation during noodle processing. Food and Science (Japan) Vol.5:108.

Wu, T.P. and Kuo, W.T. (1997). The Effects of processing parameters on quality stabilisation of frozen noodle using Taguchi quality engineering methods (to be published) C.G.P.R.D.I. Taipei.

Wu, T.P. and Kuo, W. (1997). Technical report of nonfried instant noodle unpublished C.G.P.R.D.I. Taipei.

Yano, T. (1988). The science and engineering of air-bubble dispersion system in "Emulsion and Dispersion" P65-103. Toshimasa Yano ed. Kohrin. Tokyo.

Evaluating the End-Use Quality of Wheat Breeding Lines for Suitability in Asian Noodles

Craig F. Morris

U.S. Dept. of Agriculture, Agricultural Research Service, Western Wheat Quality Laboratory, Pullman, Washington, USA

Introduction

To produce high quality noodle products that appeal to consumers of the Pacific Rim, noodle manufacturers must have a consistent supply of high quality flour. Moving "up stream" from the noodle manufacturer logically involves the flour miller, the grain merchandiser and shipper, the farmer and eventually the plant breeder. A primary concern of the Western Wheat Quality Laboratory is the evaluation of thousands of wheat breeding lines each year for their end-use quality, or *suitability*, in several important food categories, one such category being Asian noodles. Asian noodles are by no means a single entity; there is a vast array of noodle types consumed throughout Asia with many local variations. Naturally, some noodles are very similar to one another while others are distinctly different. To determine the suitability of a given wheat breeding line for one or more noodle types, we define a limited number of more general types along with their important quality criteria. We recognise the following general types: white salted Japanese *Udon*, Korean dried white salted, instant (fried, *ie.* ramen or cup), *Hokkien* par-boiled alkaline, fresh or wet Cantonese alkaline, and alkaline egg noodle such as Thailand Bamee. For each of these general types, three key quality traits are emphasised and evaluated. These traits include, gluten strength, starch pasting quality, and colour (stability, reaction, etc.). Each trait will be dealt with individually.

Gluten Strength

For most noodles, a moderate level of gluten strength is desired, neither too strong, nor too weak. However, the relative importance of gluten strength varies considerably. Noodle manufacturers have essentially identified fairly specific levels of protein content, given one or more traditional market classes of the major exporting countries of the world, that produce satisfactory end-product. For example, for a *Hokkien* noodle in Taiwan,

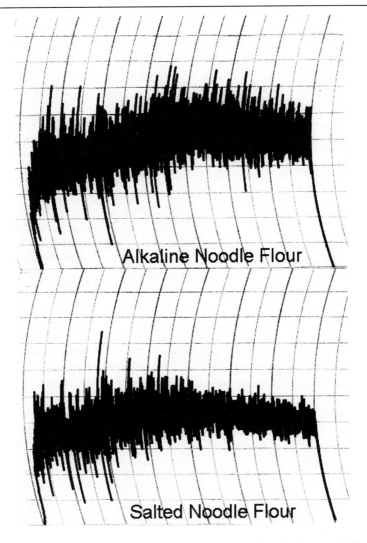

Figure 1. Ten-gram mixograms of *Seifun* Chinese alkaline noodle flour (left, 64% water absorption @ 14% flour moisture basis; 11.2% protein, 0.32% ash) and Showa *Udon* (salted) noodle flour (right, 60% water absorption @ 14% flour moisture basis; 8.9% protein, 0.32% ash). Flours were kindly provided by Nisshin Flour Milling Co. and Showa Sangyo, respectively.

gluten strength and the texture it imparts is the primary quality criterion. Consequently, a high protein strong gluten wheat typical of U.S. Dark Northern Spring or Canadian Western Red Spring provides the desired firmness of bite. Conversely, gluten strength for the Japanese *Udon* manufacturer is secondary to starch quality and the lower protein, weaker gluten properties of the Western Australia noodle segregation is appropriate for this noodle type.

Gluten properties are evaluated by traditional means: Mixograph (Figure 1), Farinograph, Extensigraph, Alveograph and other rheological instruments. Protein content, is measured by either Kjeldahl or Dumas, or predicted using Near Infrared Reflectance or Near Infrared Transmittance Spectroscopy. As with nearly all end-products (breads, noodles, cookies, cakes), a laboratory-scale method generally provides the best overall prediction of commercial product quality.

Starch Pasting Quality

Starch pasting quality is the primary trait responsible for the quality of Japanese and Korean white salted noodles. Research has shown that a single homoeologous gene series has a very pronounced effect on starch quality; this gene is referred to as "waxy" based on the waxy phenotype seen originally in maize kernels. Waxy wheat, like true waxy grains of other cereals, contains less than 1% amylose and therefore starch granules are comprised essentially of only amylopectin. A somewhat unique feature of wheat compared with the other major cereal crops is the allohexaploid nature of its genome ($2n = 42$; AABBDD); hence the waxy genes exist in a homoeologous series of three (Figure 2). This hexaploid genome of wheat also allows for the independent segregation of all three waxy loci such that "partially waxy" wheat grain with "reduced" amylose, or in other words, amylose levels intermediate between completely waxy (< 1%) and "normal" wheat (~22-24%) (Zeng *et al.* 1997) are possible and are, in fact, fairly common. Waxy alleles (*wx*) at either the A or B locus form the foundation and processing advantage of the very successful noodle segregation in Western Australia, based originally on the variety Gamenya.

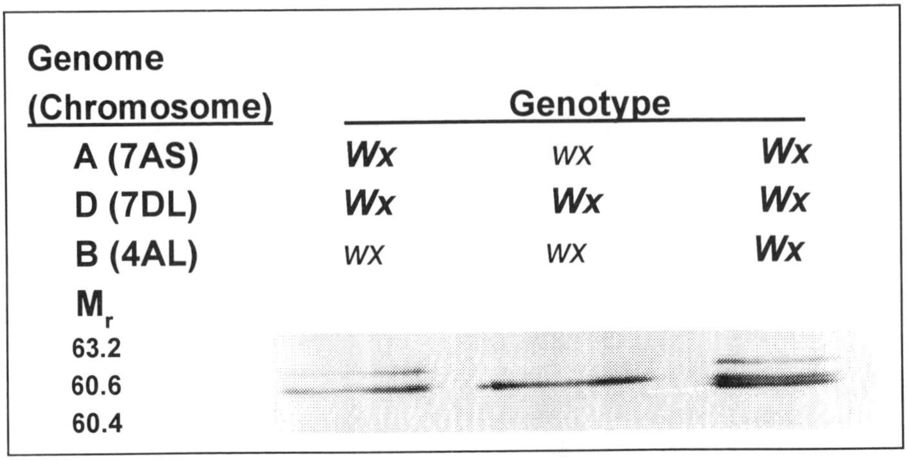

Genome (Chromosome)	Genotype		
A (7AS)	*Wx*	wx	*Wx*
D (7DL)	*Wx*	*Wx*	*Wx*
B (4AL)	wx	wx	*Wx*
M_r			
63.2			
60.6			
60.4			

Figure 2. Waxy wheat genotype and relationship with granule bound starch synthase isozymes. The waxy genes are present in a triplicated homoeologous series associated with the A, B and D genomes and located on chromosome arms 7AS, 4AL and 7DL, respectively (Nakamura *et al.* 1993). The genotypes of "Penawawa", a "one-gene waxy" typical of reduced amylose, high quality *Udon* noodle wheats (left-most lane, null for Wx-B1), "Kanto 107", a "two-gene" waxy Japanese breeding line (middle lane, null for Wx-A1 and Wx-B1), and a "normal" wild-type wheat typical of "Chinese Spring" and most cultivars (right-most lane), and the corresponding SDS-PAGE separation of GBSS isozymes are shown. The isozymes exhibit apparent molecular weights (M_r) of 63.2, 60.6, and 60.4 kDa.

There are three primary means of detecting the presence of a waxy allele. They are:

1) genotyping based on the absence of granule bound starch synthase (GBSS) isozyme in SDS polyacrylamide gel electrophoresis (SDS PAGE) gel (Figure 2);

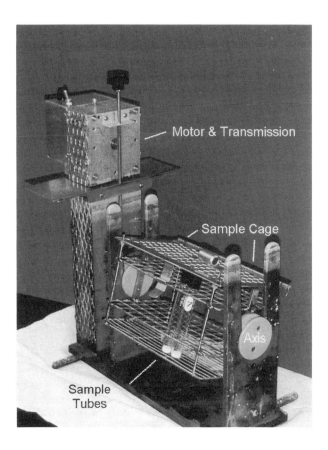

Figure 3. Machine developed by the WWQL to semi-automate the flour swelling volume test of Crosbie and co-workers (Crosbie *et al.* 1992). The procedure involves an initial rapid manual inversion of the sample cage for 2 min followed by engagement of the mechanical drive and transmission system which rotates the sample cage at 4 rpm for the remainder of the 30 min test. The entire mechanism resides in a 92.5°C water bath at a depth sufficient to completely cover the sample cage. The sample cage rotates on nylon wheels (axis) in an aluminium cradle and can be removed for tube loading and removal. Generally, 48 samples are run per batch with about 3 batches per day.

2) evaluating the empirical starch swelling capacity of starches, flours or whole-grain meals;

3) rheological measurements of gelatinised starch using instruments such as the Rapid Visco Analyser or ViscoAmylograph.

At the WWQL we use a combination of all three methods, SDS PAGE to a much lessor extent compared with the other two. Resolution of GBSS isozymes via SDS PAGE in combination with silver staining (Figure 2) is sufficiently sensitive so as to allow analyses on individual half seeds (thereby reserving the embryo portion for propagation, if desired).

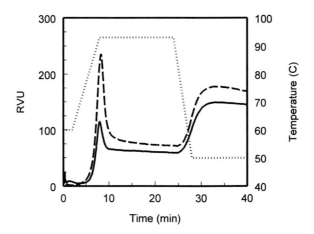

Figure. 4. Example Rapid Visco Analyser traces of a "one-gene" waxy wheat flour (– –) and a "normal" amylose type (—). The temperature program is provided (⋯⋯). For routine evaluation of breeding lines, an abbreviated temperature regimen is used: beginning temperature of 60°C during the rapid initial (10-sec) sample mixing and then heating at the maximal rate to 93°C. The sample is held at 93°C until a clearly discernable peak is obtained, upon which the peak paste viscosity is recorded and the test is terminated.

We have developed a semi-automated version of the Flour Swelling Volume (FSV) test of Crosbie and co-workers (*see* Morris *et al*. 1997 and Figure 3) to screen early-generation breeding lines, typically from F_3 headrows, preliminary yield trials, and replicated yield trials (F_5 or F_6). At this later stage of variety development (replicated yield trial) through to variety release, we employ the RVA and two specific temperature regimens (Figure 4). Uncharacterised varieties or research material are generally evaluated using the "full" heating and cooling regimen so as to obtain the full gelatinisation and gelation curve.

Colour

Colour is of paramount importance to most all Asian noodles. Obviously, it is the first quality attribute perceived by the consumer. In judging wheat breeding lines as to their suitability in alkaline noodles of the *Hokkien* and Cantonese types, we place colour, or more specifically colour stability, as the number one quality criterion. We further consider the "raw" or "fresh" Cantonese type as being the more demanding for colour stability since it receives no partial cooking prior to sale. Cooking is an important consideration because by far the biggest concern is with the development of ***bad*** colour, in other words, colour deterioration, or poor *colour stability*. Cooking can have a major influence in halting or ameliorating the development of poor colour. Is has been suggested by numerous researchers that polyphenol oxidase is the primary culprit in the development of bad colours, usually dark browns or greys. Our data suggest that a major component of this discolouration may reside on the group 2 chromosomes (J.V. Anderson, *pers. comm.*). Morris, Jeffers and Engle of the WWQL have developed a robust small-scale test method for predicting the colour of alkaline noodles. The method employs 100 g of flour, *kan sui* solution, and the common pin-type Swanson-Working mixer (such as supplied by National Manufacturing Co. and used in the AACC "pup" loaf bread method) (AACC 1995). Doughs are sheeted with the Ohtake sheeter, and measured with the Minolta Chroma Meter at both 0 and 24 hr. To date, we have emphasised high L* values at 24 hr, since a bright, stable colour seems to be universally preferred. Figure 5 shows typical results for a variety with "bad" and one with "good" colour over a number of environments, locations and crop years. Obviously, this colour parameter is highly influenced by genotype.

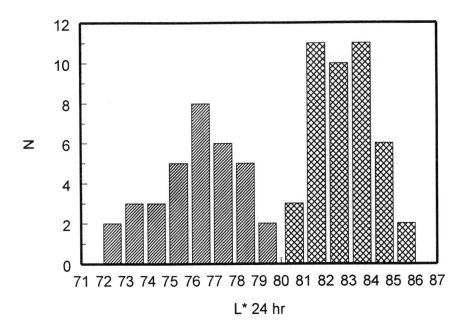

Figure 5. Histogram of L* values of raw alkaline noodle sheets at 24 hr prepared from various samples of "Eltan" (cross-hatched) and "Klasic" (striped) white wheats, n = 43 and 34, respectively. The two populations were non-overlapping. L* was measured using the CR-310 Minolta Chroma Meter on 1 mm-thick sheet with a white tile background.

Secondary Considerations

We consider the most important "secondary trait" to be grain hardness. Generally speaking, wheats for Japanese *Udon* and Korean white salted noodles are preferred to be soft-textured, whereas most alkaline noodles are currently made from hard wheats. This preference, at least in the case of some alkaline noodles, may be an artefact of the breeding and class systems in the major exporting countries where hard grain and strong gluten generally go hand-in-hand. Stronger-gluten soft white wheats with exceptionally good brightness have received very favourable evaluations by Asian noodle and mill technicians (M. Kruk, *pers. comm.*). Certainly, the same universal considerations of milling performance, starch damage, flour particle size distribution, etc., will still hold true. Additionally, such issues as water absorption, starch damage, sheeting and dough handling, and noodle surface properties will be influenced by grain hardness.

The other secondary trait worthy of mention is grain colour. For noodles, white grain, *ie.* white bran, is universally preferred. In white salted noodles and other types prepared at near-neutral pH, bran contamination is less of a colour problem and extraction may be increased with white wheats. In alkaline noodles, red bran is particularly troublesome, because red bran turns a pronounced dark brown at higher pH's and makes for overall poorer colour as well as speck problems.

Conclusion

In conclusion, the multitude of different types of noodles consumed in Asia may be reduced to a few general types which share common quality attributes. These quality attributes guide the WWQL in identifying which wheat breeding lines may be suitable for a particular noodle product. The main underlying criteria include primarily gluten strength, starch pasting quality and alkaline colour stability, and secondarily, grain hardness and bran colour.

Acknowledgments

I would like to thank Art Bettge for expert assistance in the preparation of this manuscript, and Mark Kruk for critically reviewing the paper for content. Also, many thanks to the staff and former students, postdoctoral fellows, and visiting scientists for the success of the program at the WWQL. Special thanks to CEBP, Ltd.

References

AACC. 1995. Approved methods of the American Association of Cereal

Chemists, 9th edn. AACC, St. Paul, MN.

Crosbie, G. B., W. J. Lambe, H. Tsutsui, and R. F. Gilmour. 1992. Further evaluation of the flour swelling volume test for identifying wheats potentially suitable for Japanese noodles. J. Cereal Sci. 15:271-280.

Morris, C. F., B. J. Shackley, G. E. King, and K. K. Kidwell. 1997. Genotypic and environmental variation for flour swelling volume in wheat. Cereal Chem. 74:16-21.

Zeng, M., C. F. Morris, I. L. Batey, and C. W. Wrigley. 1997. Sources of variation for starch gelatinisation, pasting and gelation properties in wheat. Cereal Chem. 74:63-71.

Screening of Australian Wheat for the Production of Instant Noodles

M. Nasir Azudin
Academy of Grain Technology, Werribee, Vic, Australia

Noodles are one of the oldest forms of processed food consumed in the Asian region. Originating from China, they have evolved into many different forms with different degrees of processing complexities. Noodles can be made from a mixture of different raw material such as rice, wheat, buckwheat, mung bean, sweet potato, tapioca, sago and potato starches. With wheat flour as raw material, noodles have further diversified into many different types such as yellow alkaline noodles and Cantonese egg noodles of China and South East Asia, *ramen* and *udon* noodles of Japan, white salted noodles of Korea and the modern day instant noodles.

Origin of instant noodles

The modern day instant noodles originated from Japan. Momofuku Ando in his book "Rising to the Challenge" described his personal experience in the research and development of instant noodle for the Japanese market (Ando, 1992). The impetus behind the development of instant noodles was the need for quick preparation of ramen to cater for the long lines of people at the noodle stalls of post war Japan. Chicken ramen launched in 1958 was the first instant food product commercialized in Japan. The large-scale production and mass marketing of instant noodles in Japan coincided with the opening of supermarket chains, distribution links and advertising through television. In 1958, Nissin Food Product produced 13 million packs of instant noodles.

Instant noodles can now be found in most supermarkets all over the world. Currently, about 40% of wheat used in the production of noodles are used for the manufacture of instant noodles. Major instant noodle manufacturers include Nissin Food Products (Japan), Myojo Food Co. (Japan), P.T Indofood Sukses Makmur (Indonesia), Nestle' S.A. (Switzerland), Nong Shim Co. (South Korea), President Enterprises Corp. (Taiwan), Campbell Soup Co (USA) and Universal Robina Corp. (Philippines).

There are many reasons for the increasing popularity of instant noodles, the main reason being convenience. Most forms of noodles require more than three to five minutes of cooking time. The thicker *udon* noodles (> 4mm thick) require about 15 to 20 minutes to cook. Instant noodles on the other hand require only 1 to 2 minutes to cook.

Ease of preparation is another reason for the popularity of instant noodles. Instant noodles, commonly in the form of a noodle block, only require cooking in boiling water. The introduction of cup noodles (instant noodles in Styrofoam cups) further simplifies this by the mere addition of hot water into the cup without further boiling. Other advantages offered by instant noodles include light weight, long shelf life, relatively low cost and the availability of a wide range of flavours with the noodles. Instant noodles make a popular snack food or even a meal for many consumers all over the world.

Production and consumption of instant noodles

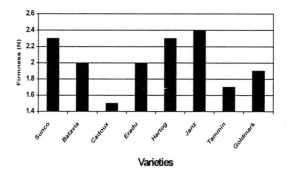

Figure 1. Global production of instant noodles.

Instant noodles come in different forms and shapes to suit the requirements of consumers (Miskelly, 1993; Kim, 1996). Bag-type instant noodles are either square or round in shape. The noodle strands vary in thickness and width, ranging from 1.2mm to 1.9mm for thickness and 1.4mm to 2.9mm width. The cross sectional area of the noodles contributes to the overall rate of cooking in the processing line and the rehydration rate of noodles prior to eating. Cup type instant noodles served in a plastic or a Styrofoam cup are normally less than 1 mm in diameter, in order to facilitate the rate of rehydration of noodles at low water temperatures (less than $100^{o}C$).

The production of instant noodles has increased dramatically in the last decade (Figure 1). The world production has increased from 15.2 billion packets in 1990 to over 40 billion packets in 1996 (Anon, 1997). This increase in production is facilitated by the introduction of improved automated production lines, packaging and distribution systems. Instant noodle factories can now be found in many countries in Asia, Australia, India, Africa, Middle East, Europe and America.

Table 1 shows the consumption trend of instant noodles in various countries of the world. China is the highest consumer of instant noodles (15 billion packs) followed by Indonesia (8 billion packets). Japan consumes about 5.3 billion packets per annum while consumption in Korea is about 3.7 billion packets in 1996 (Anon, 1997).

Although China is the largest consumer of instant noodles in the world, its per capita consumption is relatively small compared to other countries (<15 packets per capita per annum). Korea has the highest per capita consumption of instant noodles (>78 packets) (Kim, 1997). Per capita consumption of instant noodles for other countries is 41 for Japan, 40 for Indonesia and less than 6 packets of instant noodle per capita for Australia (Anon, 1997)

Table 1. Consumption of instant noodles in different countries (100 millions packets).

Country	1990	1992	1993	1994	1995	1996
Japan	46.0	48.7	50.2	50.4	52.0	53.0
South Korea	38.0	36.1	35.6	37.1	35.2	37.3
China	14.0	13.0	30.0	40.2	132.7	150.0
Taiwan	5.5	6.7	7.3	7.8	8.1	8.4
Thailand	7.5	5.5	9.5	12.0	13.4	13.4
Indonesia	17.0	47.6	56.0	70.0	76.5	79.7
Malaysia	2.0	2.0	3.0	3.0	3.3	3.6
USA	12.0	14.0	15.3	18.0	20.0	20.0

Benchmarking of commercial instant noodles

In order to screen and select correct wheat types for the production of instant noodles, it is important to understand the quality characteristics of instant noodles. Benchmarking of commercial instant noodles is the best way to understand the quality requirements of instant noodles. Studies on commercial instant noodles from various part of the world indicated a wide range of quality characteristics (Azudin *et al.*, 1997a). These differences are partly due to the type of wheat supplied by the different flourmills in the region but mainly due to preferences of consumers in the region

Table 2. Physical and chemical composition of commercial instant noodles.

Country	Weight/g	% protein	% ash	% fat
China	65 - 100g	7 – 12.1	1.5-3.0	17-22
Indonesia	65 – 125g	9.7 – 11.8	1.1-1.9	16.1-20.6
Malaysia	80 – 85g	8.5 – 10.5	2.1-3.0	17.7
Thailand	~60g	7.7 – 10.8	2.4-3.0	20.6
Korea	120 – 130g	7.5 – 8.1	1.2-1.7	12-20
Taiwan	~95g	~9.8	2.4	21
Singapore	~85g	~9.0	1.6	20.2
Philippines	50-65g	9.8 – 10.2	0.7-2.0	19-24
Vietnam	~85g	7.4 – 8.8	2.5-3.3	18-20

Noodle weight and type

Apart from different shape of noodle block, instant noodles are sold in different weights, ranging from as little of 40g to 130g. Instant noodle blocks, commonly found in Asia are normally about 65g to 85g in weight (Table 2). Instant noodles sold in Korea however, are normally about 120g in weight, indicating a more substantial meal compared to those found in other regions. This difference in size can be attributed to the way instant noodles are consumed in the various countries. In most regions, instant noodles are consumed as a snack between meals, with nothing more than the flavour provided in the packets. In Korea, however instant noodles are consumed more like a meal with the addition of freeze-dried vegetables and seafood. This consumption pattern has an important significance to the future consumption trend of instant noodles. A change in the consumption pattern of instant noodles (from a snack to a meal), will significantly increase the requirement of wheat for the production of this product. It is also reported that there is an increase in the consumption of cup type instant noodles and a reduction in the consumption of bag-type instant noodles (Kim, 1997). This is due to the increased convenience provided by cup-type instant noodles.

Protein content

Protein content of flour plays an important role in determining the firmness of noodles (Gore *et al.*, 1988). High protein flour tends to produce noodles of firm texture. Survey on the protein content of commercial instant noodles showed that the protein levels ranged from 7 to 12 % (Table 2). This variation is due to the different wheat grist used by the various flourmills in the region and has an influence on the texture of the noodles. Instant noodle samples obtained from Indonesia are normally relatively high in protein content as compared to those obtained from Korea. Instant noodles made in Korea normally have starch added to produce the preferred texture of instant noodles for the region.

Ash content

Ash content of noodles represents the level of different mineral salts found in instant noodles. These salts are added to the instant noodles during production. Ash content is also correlated to the extraction levels of the flour used. Commercial instant noodles contain between 0.7 to 3.3% ash. Instant noodles with low ash content indicate the use of low extraction flour (<60% extraction levels) in its production (Table 2)

Fat content

Instant noodles are made through a continuous process of steaming and frying of noodles. The noodles take up some oil during the frying process so the fat content of instant noodles is relatively high. Fat content of commercial instant noodles ranged from 16% to 24% (Table 2). Instant noodles made from low protein, high starch flour normally take up more oil than those made from high protein flour (Azudin, 1997a). This increase in oil uptake is due to the increase porosity of noodle structure made from low protein flour.

Table 3. Quality characteristics of commercial instant noodles.

Country	Cooking time / min	Cooked noodle colour (L)	Cooked noodle colour (b)	Firmness of noodle strands (N)
China	1.5-5.0	65-78	25-37	1.0-1.6
Indonesia	2.0-4.0	72-77	28-32	1.2-2.1
Malaysia	3.0-3.5	71.75	22-25	1.9-2.0
Thailand	2.5-3.0	66-69	27-29	1.3-2.2
Korea	2.3-3.3	68-79	23-36	1.5-2.2
Taiwan	2.8	70	26	1.1
Singapore	2.5	72	26	1.3
Philippines	2.5-3.0	67-73	21-37	1.6-2.1
Vietnam	2.0-2.5	64-72	22-30	0.9-1.3

Cooking time

One of the main advantages of instant noodles over other type of noodle is the short cooking times. Cooking time of instant noodles normally range from 2 to 3 minutes (Table 3). Steamed and dried instant noodles normally take longer to cook (4 to 5 minutes) due to the more compact and less porous nature of the noodle strands. Cup noodles provide an additional convenience to consumers as it only requires hot water instead of boiling in a pan.

Noodle colour

Colour is one of the most important quality characteristics of noodles. Brightness and yellowness of noodles determine to some extent customer acceptance. The brightness and yellowness of noodles are dependent on the flour and other ingredients used in the formulation and the processing conditions used in the production of noodles (Moss et al., 1986; Kruger et *al.*, 1992; Mares *et al.*, 1997). Brightness of cooked commercial instant noodles ranged from 64 to 79 on the "L*" scale. The yellowness of commercial instant noodles ranged from 22 to 36 on the "b*" scale (Table 3).

Noodle texture

Firmness of noodles constitutes one the eating quality characteristics assessed by consumers. Hard and very firm texture is not a characteristic sought after in instant noodles. Most instant noodles are moderate in firmness and slightly chewy. Table 3 compares the firmness of instant noodles from different regions. Firmness of 5 strands of commercial instant noodles ranged from 0.9 N to 2.2 N on the Lloyds texture meter.

Screening of Australian wheat varieties for the production of instant noodles

In the screening of wheat varieties for the production of instant noodles, two different target users need to be considered namely the noodle manufacturer and the consumers. The instant noodle manufacturers are concerned with the quality of the flour used in the formulation and the processing behaviour of flour during the production of instant noodles in the factory. The consumer on the other hand is interested in the eating quality of the instant noodles. The assessment of Australian wheat varieties conducted at the Academy of Grain Technology aims to cover these three aspects of quality – flour quality, processing quality and eating quality.

Assessment of flour quality

In selecting wheat varieties for instant noodles, various flour quality characteristics are assessed. These include flour colour, protein content and dough properties, starch quality and ash content.

Flour colour

The colour of instant noodles is determined by flour colour, processing method and other colouring agents added in the formulation. Flour colour is dependent on the wheat variety, extraction rates and particle size.

A combination of brightness and yellowness are the desired characteristics preferred by most consumers. Low protein, high starch flour tends to have better brightness (high "L*" values) compared to high protein flour. Flour with low milling extraction rates has better brightness compared to those at higher extractions. These produce brighter noodles, with minimum specking. Flour with high ash content produces dull, greyish noodles compared to noodles made from low ash flour which exhibits good bright appearance.

The yellowness of instant noodles is due to the inherent yellow pigments in the wheat flour and the development of yellow colour by flavonoids under alkaline condition (Miskelly, 1984; Mares, 1997). Australian wheat varieties such as Batavia, Krichauff and Rosella have high levels of carotenoids and flavonoids, producing bright yellow instant noodles.

Changes in the colour of noodle dough sheets is due to enzymatic activities of polyphenol oxidase (Lamkin *et al.*, 1981). This is more critical for raw noodles as polyphenol oxidase results in a dull, greyish noodle after 24 hours. Polyphenol oxidase activity is not crucial for instant noodle production due to the relatively short time between dough reduction and the steaming of noodle strands which inactivates the enzyme. Nonetheless, high levels of polyphenol oxidase activity would result in slight discolouration of noodles, especially under elevated temperatures (>35 $^{\circ}$C) in the factory.

Protein content and quality

Ideally, instant noodles are made from flour with protein content higher than 9%. Low protein flour produces noodles that are soft in texture and not stable in the liquid environment in which instant noodles are normally served. Instant noodles made from soft wheat also tends to be sticky during the steaming process due to the collapsing of noodle waves, blocking the flow of steam through the noodles in the steaming tunnel. Very strong flour with low extensibility is not suitable for instant noodles. This flour tends to produce dough sheets that shrink after each compression stage and therefore require additional compression.

Starch quality

Starch plays an important role in the texture of noodles. The gelatinisation and swelling of starch during cooking makes up the bulk of the noodle structure. Although protein plays an important role during processing and handling of dough, starch on the other hand plays an important role in the final texture of noodles. Flour with high starch paste viscosity results in noodles of increased chewiness. However, high starch paste viscosity may result in slight softening of the noodles, through increased porosity of noodle strands and increased absorption of water during boiling and in the soup.

Assessment on the processing quality of flour

The behaviour of flour during the processing of instant noodles is of great importance to noodle manufacturers. The ease of handling and the consistency of processing behaviour of flour in a high-automated processing environment determine the acceptance of a particular wheat grist in the manufacture of instant noodles. Screening of suitable wheat varieties should therefore include an assessment on the processing behaviour of wheat varieties during the various stages in the production of instant noodles. Fig.2 outlines the different processing stages in the manufacture of instant noodles. This section will further describe the processing and assessment of flour during the production of instant noodles using a pilot scale instant noodle plant at the Academy of Grain Technology in Melbourne, Australia. The procedure described below follows closely industrial methods of production.

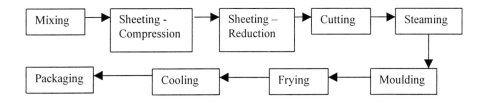

Figure 2. Process flow in the production of instant noodles.

Mixing of noodle flour

All ingredients other than flour are dissolved in water prior to mixing. This is then added to the wheat flour and mixed (Table 4). In the manufacture of noodles, the mixing stage is conducted in order to achieve a uniform distribution of various ingredients in the flour and to hydrate the flour particles.

Table 4. Basic formulation for instant noodles.

Ingredients	Amount (%)
Flour	100
Water	32-35
Salt	1
Alkaline salt (potassium carbonate : sodium carbonate at 6:4)	1

During the mixing of noodle flour, hydration of flour protein occurs, resulting in the formation of small dough crumbs. The size of the dough crumbs varies with different flour types. Figure 3 shows the crumb size distribution of noodle dough made from flour of different protein content. The crumb size ranged from <1mm in diameter to >8mm in diameter (Azudin *et al.*, 1997c) The crumb distribution is correlated to protein content and starch damage. High protein flour tends to produce larger crumbs compared to low protein flour. Commercial mixers normally produce noodle dough crumbs as big as 3 cm in diameter.

Flour with high levels of starch damage also produce large sticky crumbs. These are normally sticky on the outside and usually produce uneven hydration on the noodle dough. Crumb size is important in the production of noodle dough sheets. Large, sticky crumbs produce uneven dough sheets, which require additional sheeting stages. Large crumbs of uneven hydration result in uneven formation and development of gluten during the sheeting stages, which subsequently result in tearing of dough sheets.

Sheeting of noodle dough

The crumbly noodle dough is developed during the sheeting process. Here the crumbly dough is compressed between a series of rollers. The initial 2 sets of roller compresses the crumbly dough into a thick dough sheet. This is then further compressed through a series of six rollers at decreasing roller gaps. Figure 4 shows the series of reduction rollers used in the development of noodle dough for the production of instant noodles. Noodle dough sheet is fed between each roller. A frequency modulator regulates the speed of the rollers in order not to stretch the dough sheet.

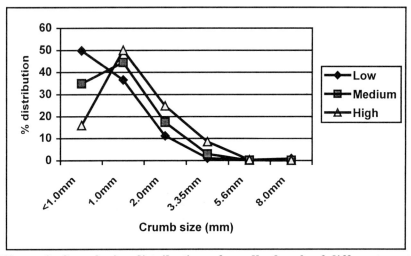

Figure 3. Crumb size distribution of noodle dough of different protein content.

Quality assessment of the dough sheet at this stage includes evaluation of the appearance and handling characteristics of the dough. The dough sheet should not be streaky. Streakiness indicates uneven mixing and hydration, which will result in uneven development of gluten. Since a dough-resting stage is not normally practiced in a commercial plant, uneven hydration of gluten will normally result in weak points along the length of the noodle strands. These eventually result in breakage of the noodle strands during packaging and transportation.

Dough development is achieved during the compression and reduction of the noodle dough sheet. Studies on work input have show different energy requirements for the development of noodle dough sheets during compression (David *et al.*, 1997; Edwards, *et al.*, 1996). As the noodle dough sheet gets reduced, a continuous protein matrix is formed (Moss *et al.*, 1987). Texture analysis at different spots along the noodle dough sheet have shown that the firmness of noodle dough is not consistent at the beginning of the compression stage compared to the end of the compression stage. Figure 5a shows the inconsistency in firmness of noodle dough at the early stages of compression and Figure 5b shows the reproducibility of firmness at different parts of noodle dough sheet after 5 passes through the reduction rollers (Martin and Azudin, unpublished results)

Figure 4. Reduction rollers for development of noodle dough sheets.

Stickiness of dough sheets is another important characteristic assessed during the screening of wheat varieties for the production of instant noodles. Sticky dough sheets result in tearing and folding back of the dough sheet into the roller gaps. This results in down time in the processing line. Since dusting starch is not used in an automatic instant noodle plant, sticky dough sheet is a characteristic not acceptable to noodle manufacturers.

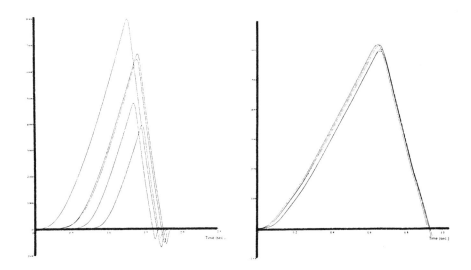

Figure 5. Firmness of noodle dough sheet measured with a TA-XT2 Analyser after 1 (left) and 5 (right) passes through reduction rollers.

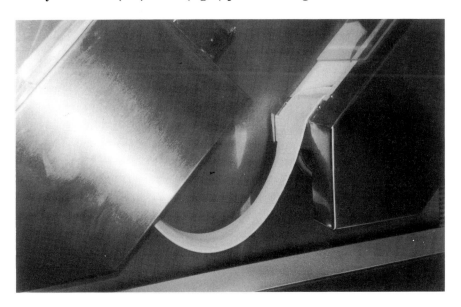

Figure 6. Slack of dough sheet between reduction rollers.

Extensibility of dough is important for the manufacture of noodle. However, very extensible dough results in slacking of dough sheets between rollers (Figure 6). This results in thinner dough sheets, which will affect the weight of noodle blocks. A rotating blade controlled by timing gears cuts the noodle blocks. Thinner noodle strands will result in noodle blocks with lighter final weight. A soft, extensible dough sheet also results in tearing of sheets. Strong, dough with low extensibility, on the other hand results in shrinking of the dough sheet during reduction. Strong doughs cause problems in achieving correct dough thickness prior to cutting of the dough sheet.

Colour of noodle sheets are measured after the reduction process. This is carried out using the Minolta CR310 Colour meter with a 50mm diameter aperture. The noodle sheet is folded and placed on a standard white tile before colour measurement is taken (Figure 7).

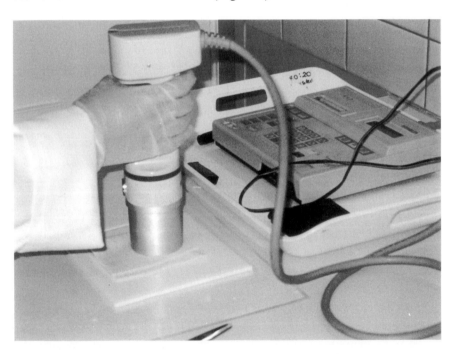

Figure 7. Measurement of noodle sheet colour.

Cutting of noodle dough

Noodle sheets are normally cut using a 1mm cutter. The flow of noodle strands emerging from the cutter are hindered by metal blocks, resulting in the noodle waves, unique to instant noodles (Figure 8). Good gluten development is essential during cutting of noodle sheets. Dry noodle dough sheet results in breakage during cutting and the formation of loose crumbs which eventually clog up the system.

Figure 8. Cutting of noodle strands before entering the steaming tunnel.

Steaming of instant noodles

Instant noodles are steamed in a steaming tunnel where they are partially gelatinised. Degree of gelatinisation achieved during steaming is an important quality characteristic. A higher degree of gelatinisation of noodle strands in the steaming tunnel is preferred.

Frying of instant noodles

Partially cooked instant noodles are cut into blocks by a rotating blade and moulded into a moulder. Noodles are then fried in palm oil for 60 sec. at 150°C. Noodles are assessed based on their appearance at the end of the frying process. An additional brown colour develops during the frying process during to Maillard reaction and caramelisation of sugars. This is more pronounced in noodle flour with high sugar or damaged starch.

Assessment of the quality of instant noodles.

In addition to the processing behaviour of noodle flour, the final quality of resultant instant noodles is assessed for their appearance and eating quality. The instant noodles are cooked and the colour of noodles measured using the Minolta CR310 Colour meter equipped with a 50mm diameter aperture. Sufficient cooked noodles are place in a bowl and the colour reading is taken directly on the noodles. Figure 9 shows the colour of noodles made from different Australian wheat varieties.

Figure 9 shows a great variation in the colour of instant noodles made from different wheat varieties. Sunco is the least yellow while Goldmark and Batavia are amongst the yellowest of the samples tested.

The eating quality of instant noodles can be assessed objectively or subjectively. Objective measurement of noodle firmness can be achieve by using texture meters such as the Instron Universal Texture meter, TA-TX2 Texture analyser or the Lloyds Texture meter (Oh *et al.*, 1983; Karim (1990). Figure 10 shows the measurement of noodle firmness using the Lloyds texture meter. Noodles are placed on a platform and are then cut using a flat blade and the resistance to strain measured.

Figure 11 above shows the firmness of instant noodles made from different Australian wheat flour. Soft wheat such as Cadoux and Tammin produced soft instant noodles while the hard grain varieties of Hartog, Janz and Sunco produced noodles of firmer texture. As explained earlier, the preferred texture of noodles varies with different consumer groups. There is on one wheat variety with the ideal texture. Understanding the customer requirement through both objective and subjective assessment of texture will allow for better blending of different wheat grist to produce the ideal texture characteristics for the target consumer.

Figure 12 shows the surface structure of instant noodles. The surface is uneven and has numerous pores. These pores are produced during the frying stage of production. Water in the noodle strands, is driven out at high temperature during the frying stage, creating these tiny pores. Swollen starch granules that have dislodged themselves from the surface of the noodles during frying could also produce these pores. These pores provide space for oil uptake during frying. They also create the porous structure in the noodle strands which allows quicker rehydration prior to consumption.

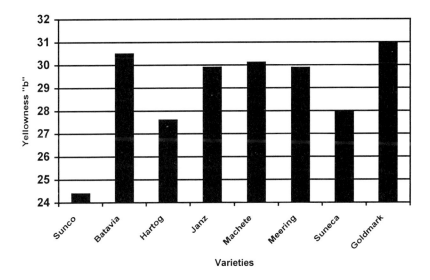

Figure 9. Yellowness of instant noodles made from different wheat varieties.

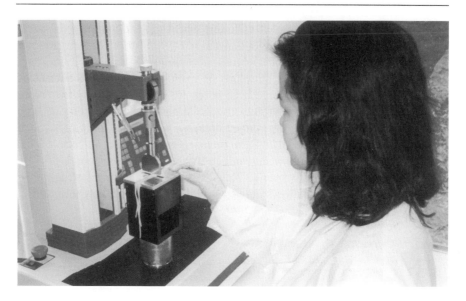

Figure 10. Measurement of noodle firmness using a texture meter.

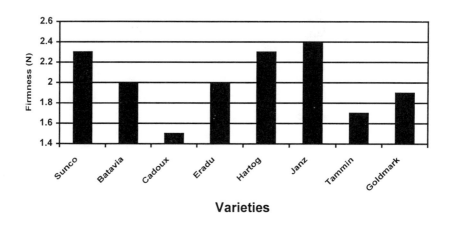

Figure 11. Firmness of instant noodles made from different wheat varieties.

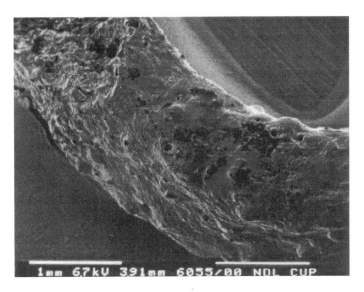

Figure 12. Scanning electron microgram of an instant noodle strand.

Further work

Assessment of the processing quality and eating quality of noodles is important in the selection and screening of suitable wheat varieties. These tests are however fairly subjective. There is a need for the development of quick and simple quantitative measurement of these qualities. Quantification and monitoring of noodle dough development, on-line measurement of degree of gelatinisation and objective measurements of noodle texture (firmness and chewiness) are some of the assessment methods needed which will allow for more effective screening of wheat varieties.

References.

Anon (1997). *National trend in instant ramen demand* by International RAMEN Manufacturers Association (IRMA)

Ando, M (1993) *Rising to the Challenge*. Foodeum Communication, Tokyo, Japan.

Azudin, M. N. (1997a). Pages 111-113 in Proc. 47th Aust. Cereal Chem. Conf. Royal Australian Chemical Institute, Melbourne, Australia.

Azudin, M. N. (1997b). Pages 299-303 in Proc. 47th Aust. Cereal Chem. Conf. Royal Australian Chemical Institute, Melbourne, Australia

Azudin, M. N. (1997c). Pages 118-122 in Proc. 47th Aust. Cereal Chem. Conf. Royal Australian Chemical Institute, Melbourne, Australia.

Edwards, N.M., Scanlon, M.G., Kruger, J.E. and Dexter, J.E. (1996) Cereal Chem. 73, 708-711.

Gore, P.J., Miskelly, D.M. and Moss, H.J. (1988) Pages 97-102 in Proc. 38th Aust. Cereal Chem. Conf. Royal Australian Chemical Institute, Melbourne, Australia

Karim, R. (1990) Textural studies on Chinese wet noodles (Hokkien style noodles). Thesis, Universiti Pertanian Malaysia.

Kim, S.K (1996) Pages 195-225 in *Pasta and Noodle Technology*. Ed. Kruger J.E and Matsuo R.B and Dick J.W.

Kim, S.K. (1997) Pages 96-99 in Proc. 47th Aust. Cereal Chem. Conf. Royal Australian Chemical Institute, Melbourne, Australia

Kruger, J.E., Matsuo, R.B. and Preston, K. (1992) Canadian J. Plant Sci. 72 (1021-1029)

Lamkin, W.M., Miller, B.S., Nelson, S.W., Taylor, D.D. and Lee, M.S. (1981) Cereal Chem. 58:27-31.

Martin, D.M., Azudin, M.N. and Stewart, B.G. (1997). Pages 106-110 in Proc. 47th Aust. Cereal Chem. Conf. Royal Australian Chemical Institute, Melbourne, Australia.

Miskelly, D.M. (1984) J. Sci. Food Agric. 35:463-471.

Miskelly, D.M. (1985) J. Cereal Sci. 3:379-387.

Miskelly, D.M. (1993) Food Australia 45 (10), 496-500.

Mares, D. J., Wang, Y and Cassidy, C.A. (1997). Pages 114-117 in: Proc. 47th Aust. Cereal Chem. Conf. Royal Australian Chemical Institute, Melbourne, Australia.

Modern noodle based foods - raw material needs

D M Miskelly
Goodman Fielder Milling and Baking, Summer Hill, NSW, Australia

Noodles have long been considered as a staple food in the diet of many Asian peoples. Rising living standards in Asia and the Pacific Rim in recent years have lead to an increased consumption of wheat based foods, particularly noodles. Sales of instant noodles in countries in the Pacific rim doubled in the decade to 1995/96 to an estimated 30 billion units (Anon. 1997a).

Asian noodles can be based on wheat flour, rice flour, buckwheat flour or starches derived from rice, wheat, mung bean, tapioca, sweet potato and corn, but only those noodles based on wheat flour will be considered in this paper. There are a number of different types of wheaten noodles and a variety of processing methods. Some generalised classification is possible on the basis of different raw materials, processing and size and shape of the finished noodles (Nagao, 1996; Miskelly 1996). The most common types of wheat flour based noodles in Asia are white salted noodles (eg Japanese *udon*, Chinese *gua mian*), yellow alkaline noodles (eg *Hokkien*, Japanese *ramen*) and instant noodles (eg Korean *ramyon* and long life noodles).

Differences in processing stages means that noodles can be sold "fresh" or "raw" (moisture content 32-38%), "boiled and then refrigerated", "boiled and frozen" (moisture content 50-60%), "semi-dried" (moisture content 20-28%), "dried" (moisture content 10-13%), "steamed" (moisture content 50-60%), "fried", "steamed and fried" (moisture content 4-8%), or "steamed and dried" (10-14%). In order to add value to the noodles, many types are included with packet soups, seasonings or toppings or sold in a cup or bowl, forming a complete meal on the addition of boiling water.

While the major raw material for wheat based noodles is flour, there are in fact many other ingredients which all contribute to the quality of the finished product, particularly in the case of instant noodles (Table 1). The quality requirements and raw material needs are quite important and precisely defined in some Pacific Rim countries but are much less important and more generally defined in others, where economic factors and the supply situation have a greater impact. The requirement for a high quality raw material specification by the manufacturer, and, indeed the high consumer expectation of the quality of that product tends to follow the degree of economic development in that country within the Asian region.

Table 1. Ingredients used in noodle production

Common ingredients	Additional ingredients
flour	egg powder
water	stabilisers (eg gums)
salt/alkaline salts	polyphosphates
eggs	carboxymethylcellulose
gluten	oil
starch	antioxidants
colourings	preservatives
	emulsifiers
	milk powder
	buckwheat
	flavourings

Consumer expectations

Consumers of all food products require fresh, safe, nutritious, high quality foods at a satisfactory price (Seneur *et al.* 1991). They are often concerned about food safety issues such as pesticides, additives and chemicals. In 1996 there was a large outbreak of food poisoning in Japan (almost 9000 reported cases) associated with *E coli 0157*. This organism is normally associated only with meat products, but following widespread consumer and Government concern at the time, importers of most food products and ingredients requested microbiological testing to confirm product safety.

Specifically, consumers of noodles expect that the product should be bright in colour and free from discolouration, have an adequate shelf life without visible microbiological deterioration, and have appropriate flavour and textural characteristics which will vary according to the noodle type and region.

Noodle manufacturer expectations

From the manufacturer's perspective, products should be of high quality, good taste, suit consumer expectations and represent value for money. They should also be nutritious, safe and conform with the relevant Food Standards for noodles in the country of sale. The raw materials manufacturers source must be suitable for production of the end product, that is, of appropriate and consistent quality, and also competitive in price, inclusive of freight and packaging costs. In practice, a specification is set up between raw material supplier and manufacturer, but this may not actually reflect the level of quality required. A typical noodle flour specification may include only protein, moisture and ash content. Some examples are given in Table 2. It is generally understood, if not stated, that the raw materials will also possess adequate functional and processing properties in order to produce a quality product.

Table 2.   Examples of wheat flour specifications for noodles

	Instant noodles (Japan)	Instant noodles (Korea)[a]	All noodles (PRC) grade I[b]	All noodles (PRC) grade II[b]	*Udon* noodles (Japan)
Moisture %	13.5-14.5	13.5-14.0	<14.5	<14.5	13.5-14.5
Protein %	9.5-10.5	8.7-9.6			8-10
Wet gluten %	29-31		>28	>26	
Ash %	<0.45	<0.44	0.47	0.64	<0.40
Farinograph water absorption %		58-61			
Farinograph stability min		7.6-8.9	>4	>3	
Viscograph maximum height BU		570-860			>700
Falling number secs			>200	>200	

Source [a] Kim 1997
[b] Huang 1996b

It is usually up to the flour miller to translate these functional and processing properties into quantitative flour quality terms. This necessitates a close and continuing interaction between the flour mill and noodle manufacturer, which may be more tenuous if a trading company acts as an intermediary in the chain. Appropriate flour quality characteristics may be judged from an understanding of product and process, or may need to be established through laboratory, pilot plant or commercial plant trials. Some flexibility is required by all parties to allow for seasonal variations and availability of appropriate wheats.

Wheat selection - noodle wheat quality

The key to finished product quality is correct wheat selection, followed by correct milling procedures. This will ensure that, given good manufacturing practice, finished noodles will be of high quality.

Wheats to be milled for noodle flours are assessed in terms of wheat bran colour (red or white), class, variety, protein content, hardness, moisture content, test weight/grain size, screenings, freedom from disease and soundness. There may be additional requirements such as maximum or nil chemical residues, or that the wheat has been certified as organically grown. While some of these properties such as grain colour or hardness are inherent, others such as protein content, soundness and residues are affected by seasonal, environmental or storage conditions.

Wheat colour

There is a preference for white wheats for noodle production, as judged from the popularity of Australian white wheats and the recent focus of US breeding and segregation efforts on the development of white wheats for the Asian region (Anon. 1997b). Noodles manufactured from flour milled from white wheats tend to show lower levels of discolouration with time, resulting in longer saleable product life. This is thought to be due to higher levels of polyphenol oxidases (PPO) in red wheats when compared with white wheats, although there are considerable genotypic and environmental influences in the population range (McCallum and Walker 1990; Baik *et al.* 1994; Park *et al.* 1997).

Wheat class and variety

Most flour mills will buy wheat on a grade or class basis. This ensures certain minimum specified quality criteria such as test weight, protein content and screenings level have been met. Wheat grades or classes contain mixtures of varieties, usually of similar or complimentary quality. If specific varietal characteristics such as starch pasting properties, or noodle sheet colour stability are required, it may be advantageous to source single varieties, enabling superior product characteristics.

Protein content

Wheats will be blended prior to milling to achieve the correct protein level in the flour. There is generally a drop of 1-1.5% in protein content from wheat to finished flour, so allowance is made for this in gristing. Protein content influences many of the textural and cooking properties of noodles and so is perhaps the most important wheat quality factor to be considered.

Grain hardness

Grain hardness is important in terms of wheat conditioning levels and times, milling performance and level of starch damage in the resultant flour. There is a preference for soft or semi-soft wheats for Japanese style white noodles (Nagao 1996), hard wheats for Japanese style *ramen* (Nagao 1996) and hard wheats for instant noodles (Azudin 1997).

Test weight and kernel weight

Test weight or thousand kernel weight are predictors of milling yield, and are also used to exclude small, frosted, damaged, or shrivelled grains.

Screenings or unmillable material

Chaff, whiteheads, foreign seeds, small or shrivelled grains and other non-wheat foreign material must be removed prior to milling in the wheat cleaning plant and screen room, with a resultant decrease in flour yield.

Wheat should be free from mycotoxins, bunt, black tip and other grain defects.

Soundness

Noodles are sensitive to inclusion of rain-damaged (sprouted) wheats, so a typical specification for noodle wheats will include a minimum falling number of 300 sec. Noodles manufactured from rain-damaged wheats suffer a loss of quality attributes, such as inferior texture (Moss 1980, Miskelly and Moss 1985), dark and unattractive colour (Edwards *et al.* 1989, Kruger *et al.* 1992) and breakage of strands on drying (Bean *et al.* 1974).

Consistency

Flour millers require that wheat should be of consistent high quality, readily available in sufficient quantities, competitively priced, suitable for milling and should produce flour suitable for noodle production. In the Pacific Rim, many importing countries are deregulating their wheat import systems and allowing millers to become independent wheat importers. One effect of this deregulation is that mills can now focus on quality, price and delivery (Stevens 1997). In a recent survey conducted by the Exchange Consulting Group of Winnipeg, Asian and South American wheat importers selected consistency of quality from shipment to shipment as their number one priority ahead of price considerations.

Flour quality

Flour quality is usually defined in terms of protein content, ash or colour grade, starch damage, and dough strength (as measured by the mixograph, farinograph and extensograph). Most flour mills routinely use these use these tests as quality control tools for production.

However, in assessment of flour quality for noodle manufacture, many of the traditional dough tests are of limited value once general quality considerations have been met. The challenge for millers in measuring flour quality is to include those criteria that are relevant to noodle production, as well as those defining flour mill performance. In the absence of rain damage, major noodle flour requirements relate to protein (gluten) content and quality, milling yield/flour colour or ash, flour particle size, starch damage and starch properties.

Laboratory scale, end product tests of fresh/cooked noodle colour, colour stability and noodle texture should be used in conjunction with all other tests in the assessment of noodle making potential of a flour.

Table 3. Flour protein content for different noodle types

Class	Type	Flour protein content (N x 5.7) %
Alkaline noodles	High quality fresh Cantonese	12-13
	Fresh Cantonese	10-12
	Japanese *ramen*	10-12
	Dried	10-12.5
	Boiled (*Hokkien*)	9-11
Alkaline noodles (containing egg)	*Wonton*	>13
	Hong Kong noodle (Singapore)	>13
White salted noodles	Chinese (PRC)	9-11
	Fresh/boiled Japanese (eg.*Udon*) and Korean	8-10
	Dried	9.5-11
	Thailand	11
Instant noodles	Steamed and dried	9-11.5
	Steamed and fried	8.5-12.5
	Cup	10-11.5

Protein content and quality

Each type of noodle has its own optimum protein range (Table 3) and wheat grists will be blended prior to milling to achieve flours which meet the appropriate specification criteria. Protein content is positively correlated with noodle firmness (Miskelly and Moss 1985; Shelke *et al.* 1990; Huang 1996a, Gore *et al.* 1988; Azudin 1997), so a correct range of protein content is important for textural characteristics. White salted noodles are generally made from flours in the range 8-11% protein, yellow alkaline noodles from flours in the range 9-13+% protein and instant noodles from flours in the range 8.5-12.5% protein. Dried noodles generally require a higher protein content than that for fresh or boiled noodles (Kim 1997) because the noodles must be able to withstand the drying process without breakage. Protein content is particularly important for manufacturers of instant noodles, because fat uptake during frying decreases as flour protein content increases (Gore *et al.* 1988; Azudin 1997). This is an economic consideration because of the relativity in price of oil to flour.

Gluten development during the mixing of noodle doughs in incomplete and a uniform gluten matrix is only formed during the sheeting process (Moss *et al.* 1987). In the case of doughs made by hand, or using vacuum mixers, water levels are higher, and more gluten development occurs. Therefore adequate gluten strength and extensibility is required in all noodle flours. Noodle doughs must be strong enough to withstand sheeting, but not so strong as to cause tearing or breakage of the sheet or the noodle. Strength is often expressed by farinograph stability.

A good level of dough extensibility ensures that dough sheets do not shrink back during successive roll passes. Addition of salts and alkaline salts tend to toughen noodle doughs (Moss *et al.* 1986, Edwards *et al.* 1996). Work input during dough sheeting is related to mixing strength characteristics (Edwards *et al.* 1996), with higher protein flours requiring more roll compression to achieve the required final sheet thickness.

Milling yield/flour colour

Noodle colour is affected by many factors which may be broadly categorised as flour based, ingredient based and process based (Table 4). Flour colour is an important determinant of noodle colour. Generally noodles should be bright and free from discolouration and be colour stable with time after manufacture. For white salted noodles, a white or creamy colour is desirable. The level of natural yellow pigment levels (xanthophylls) of flour is highly correlated with noodle colour (Miskelly 1984), and this is wheat variety dependent (Mares 1991). For yellow alkaline noodles, a bright yellow colour is required, although the preference for the degree of colour development is regionally based. The primary component of yellow colour development in alkaline noodles is due to a pH dependent, chemically induced colour shift in water soluble flour flavonoids, with a secondary effect due to flour xanthophylls (Mares and Wang 1995). Bleaching of flour largely destroys the natural yellow pigments, and is not recommended for noodle flours.

Table 4. Factors affecting noodle colour

Flour source	Other ingredient source	Process source
extraction rate	salt/alkaline salt	no of sheeting passes
bran colour	added water level	cooking
proteins	eggs	drying
proteases	added colourings	frying oil temperature
PPO and oxidases	added gluten	packaging (eg modified atmosphere)
flour particle size	added starch	
starch damage	preservatives	
xanthophylls		
(bleaching)		

The major factor affecting noodle colour is flour extraction rate. Wheats must be free milling to ensure the cleanest flour at the highest possible extraction rate. Higher levels of bran result in darker noodles and darkening is intensified around a nucleus of non-endosperm material (Moss 1985). This is thought to be due to the action of PPO enzymes (Moss 1985; Oh 1985) which are largely located in the bran layer. Therefore, darkening increases with increasing flour extraction rate (Kruger *et al.* 1994). Subsequent cooking by boiling or steaming, frying, drying or retort pouch packaging largely inhibits the enzyme action. Modified atmosphere packaging or oxygen scavengers, which reduce the availability of oxygen to the enzymes, can also prolong the useable shelf life of fresh noodles.

In order to remove bran specks, millers can use covers as fine as 100 micron in the mill or redresser (Kotwal *et al.* 1997). A number of other milling strategies exist to assist in clean separation of bran and endosperm including two stage dampening (where wheat moisture content is low) and adjustment of break releases in the mill. In quality conscious markets, a divide flour milling system is generally used, with the patent flour yielding as little as 30-40%. The residual 2nd and 3rd grade flour will be utilised for other purposes such as lower grade all purpose flour, confectionery, plywood and feed manufacture.

Ash content is often used as measure of flour colour, but other methods favoured include colour grade, Pekar test, tristimulus colour and reflectance methods.

Table 5. Typical ash specifications for noodle flours

Noodle type	Ash content %
Japanese *udon*	0.36-0.40 [a]
Chinese style noodles (Japan)	033-0.38 [a]
White noodles China	grade 1 <0.55db[c]
	grade II <0.70db[c]
Instant noodles Korea	0.40-0.45 [b]

Source [a]	Nagao 1996
[b]	Kim 1997
[c]	Huang 1996b

Generally, the ash content of noodle flours lies in the range 0.40-0.50%, depending on type of noodle to be manufactured and regional preference. Some typical ash levels for noodle flours are given in Table 5. Straight run or reduced extraction flour can be used for wet noodles and wonton, or for fresh noodles in areas such as China, where colour stability is not so critical. In the latter instance, saleable shelf life may be less than 24 hours, after which time noodles have become dark or badly discoloured.

Flour particle size and starch damage

A relatively fine flour particle size enables even hydration during mixing and optimum, uniform gluten development during sheeting. A typical noodle flour will have less than 15% retained on 100μ sieve. However, very fine particle size flour may be indicative of high starch damage, which should be avoided, due to an increased requirement for processing water addition during mixing (Oh *et al.* 1985). Increased starch damage is also associated with poor noodle colour (Oh *et al.* 1985; Elbers *et al.* 1996) and harder texture. Farinograph water absorption is sometimes used as an indicator of starch damage, and most noodle flours fall within the range 55-65%, with the actual level dependent on noodle type and local preference.

Starch quality

The importance of the gelatinisation properties of starch isolated from flour to the physical structure and texture of white salted noodles such as *udon* was first identified by a number of researchers in the 1980's (Oda et al 1980; Moss 1980; Lee *et al.* 1987). The required soft and elastic textural properties of Japanese *udon* and Korean dried salted noodles can be best obtained from wheats with high starch paste viscosity and high swelling starch characteristics.

Much of the variation in starch paste viscosity is cultivar dependent (Morris *et al.* 1997), therefore, careful selection of wheat will enable the appropriate starch properties to be obtained. Much effort has been focussed in wheat breeding programs and a number of small scale tests such as swelling volume and the use of the Rapid Visco Analyser and have been well described in the literature. These have yet to find wide application among processors, who still specify flour viscograph, rather than starch viscograph, as their preferred method. In Japan and Korea, manufacturers of *udon* and other white salted noodles specify minimum flour peak viscosities of at least 700 BU.

Starch properties also appear to have a role in instant noodle quality and some manufacturers of instant noodles prefer flours with low gelatinisation temperatures for rapid rehydration during cooking.

Alkaline noodles do not have the same requirement for high starch paste viscosity (Miskelly and Moss 1985; Konik *et al.* 1994). In fact, Ross *et al.* (1997) have shown that noodles made from flours with high swelling starches have softer texture than those with medium to low swelling

133

starches, suggesting an interaction between starch and protein, with protein content a more useful indicator of alkaline noodle texture.

Additional requirements

Some manufacturers of fresh and long life noodles, where hygiene is of critical importance, will have requirements for microbiological limits for the flour. A total plate count of 10,000/g or less, may be specified, placing demands on incoming wheat and milling plant hygiene. Heavy metal and pesticide residue limits may also be required.

Other raw materials

Noodle manufacturers use a number of other ingredients besides flour, such as salts, gluten, starches, eggs, colourings and stabilisers (Table 1). These ingredients directly affect and modify processing characteristics, colour and textural properties of the finished products. The largest use of micro-ingredients is in instant noodle manufacture, which tends to be more production-oriented and manufacture is on a larger scale than for other noodle types. A number of traditional micro-ingredient manufacturers have established strong links with noodle manufactures within the Asia-Pacific region.

Salts

Salt (sodium chloride) or alkaline salts (eg sodium carbonate) are commonly added to noodle doughs and these two ingredients are an important point of distinction in general classification of noodle type. Alkaline salts are available in both powdered (*kan pun*) and liquid form (*kan sui*, lye water). All salts are dissolved in water before use to form a brine solution, which is added during the mixing stage.

Sodium chloride acts to toughen the doughs during mixing and sheeting, and for dried noodles, affects the rate of drying. It also prolongs shelf life by inhibiting mould growth, and decreasing PPO activity which improves colour stability. Salt is usually added to white noodles at the rate of 1-3% by flour weight, although levels outside this range can be used.

The alkaline salts act to modify processing, dough, and starch properties. Alkaline noodles have a characteristic flavour, aroma and colour, as well as a firm and elastic texture (Miskelly 1996). The most common alkaline salts used are sodium carbonate or potassium carbonate, or a mixture of the two, but combinations with a number of other alkaline salts are used, especially in instant noodle manufacture (Table 6). Occasionally, even sodium hydroxide is used, but this is illegal in many countries.

Table 6. Alkaline salts used in noodle production.

sodium carbonate
potassium carbonate
sodium tripolyphosphate
sodium metaphosphate
sodium pyrophosphate
sodium dihydrogen phosphate
sodium hydrogen phosphate
trisodium orthophosphate
potassium dihydrogen phosphate
dipotassium phosphate
tripotassium phosphate
sodium hydrogen carbonate

For *ramen*, *Hokkien* and Cantonese noodle types, alkaline salts are normally added at about 1% by flour weight, although levels of up to 1.5% can be used before dough properties are adversely affected. For instant noodles, typical addition is at about 0.2% alkaline salts by flour weight.

Starches

Starches from sources such as potato and tapioca can be added to the formulations used in white salted noodles and instant noodles. These starches have a bland taste and very white colour, the latter giving a whiter or lighter background colour to the noodles. Exotic starches enhance the functionality of the wheat flour starch and help to compensate for poor flour quality by conferring a more elastic and chewy texture. Additionally, in instant noodles, the effect of low gelatinisation temperatures, rapid swelling characteristics and high viscosity of added starches is to reduce the cooking temperature and rehydration time. Chemically modified starches are often used, because of improved gelling properties and freeze-thaw stabilities when compared with unmodified starches. This is of importance in product quality and tolerance following demanding processing stages such as freezing or heat-sterilising which occurs in long life noodles. Long life noodles have a shelf life of 5 months at ambient temperatures, and in Japan, their high quality commands a higher retail price.

The level of addition of starches in noodle formulations is 5-25%, on a flour weight basis. Typical raw material specifications relate to moisture content, pH, particle size, microbiological limits, colour, hot and cold viscosities and acetyl value for acetylated starches.

Colours

Natural and synthetic yellow colours can be used in alkaline and egg noodles to enhance their natural yellow (Table 7). Powders are dissolved in the brine solution before use. Colourings should be chosen with care, and used at the appropriate rate and in accordance with Food Regulations. Some colours are pH sensitive (eg, annatto) or light sensitive (eg, turmeric).

Typical raw material specifications can include dye content, moisture content, stability, heavy metals, microbiological standards, packaging, storage and shelf life.

Table 7. Yellow colourings commonly used in noodles in Asia

ß carotene
riboflavin
gardenia yellow
vitamin E
tumeric
annatto
tartrazine
sunset yellow

Stabilisers

Manufacturers of instant noodles commonly use stabilisers such as gums (Table 8). These function as water binders and improve rehydration characteristics during cooking, as well as improving the texture or eating quality. Some stabilisers give a firmer noodle texture, and it is claimed this may compensate for lower than ideal flour protein content (Anon. 1995). They are wet mixed in the brine solution before use. Typical specifications for stabilisers include moisture, protein and ash contents, microbiological limits, particle size, heavy metals and pH and viscosity of a standard solution.

Table 8. Typical stabilisers and usage rates in instant noodles [a]

Type	Usage rate (%w/w)
alginic acid	0.1-0.5
CMC	0.2-0.5
guar gum	0.1-1.0
PGA and blends	0.05-0.15
sodium alginate	0.1-0.15
xanthan gum and blends	0.05-0.20

[a] Source: Anon. 1995
CMC, carboxymethylcellulose
PGA, propylene glycol alginate

Oils

Instant noodles are fried in oil after cutting and steaming. The frying step reduces the moisture content, imparts flavour, adds oil and increases starch gelatinisation (Kim, 1996; Kun and Basiron, 1994).

The most common frying oils are palm oil or palm olein. Beef tallow, although previously used, has now been replaced by palm oil due to the latter's good frying performance and stability (Kun and Basiron, 1994). Instant noodles have a high fat content - about 20%, and oxidative rancidity is the major factor limiting shelf life. The shelf life of instant noodles is usually 5-6 months.

The use of antioxidants in the frying oil, either during processing, or added to the oil in the fryer is common. The major antioxidants used to inhibit oxidation are butylated hydroxyanisole (BHA), butylated hydroxytoluene (BHT), propyl gallate, tertiary butylhydroquinone (TBHQ) and natural tocopherols (Ng 1996). Of these, TBHQ has been shown to have the best antioxidant activity (Rho et al 1986) and a number of commercial tyoes exist.

Typical specifications for refined or fractionated palm oil relate to colour (Lovibond) , flavour and aroma (bland, free of rancidity and foreign odour), moisture (<0.1%), free fatty acid (<0.1%), melting point (depending on fractionation, but generally <30°C), peroxide value (<1 meq/kg) and composition (low linoleic acid).

Crude palm oil contains high levels of carotenoids. The residual yellow colour remaining in refined palm oil adds significantly to the yellow colour of instant noodles and hence the yellowness increases with increasing fat content (Azudin *et al.* 1997). In addition, frying conditions affect colour, weight gain and moisture content (Kim 1996). Oil uptake during frying is of economic importance and reference has been made previously to the relationship between protein content of the flour and oil content of the noodles. Generally, manufacturers will try to balance processing conditions and flour protein content to achieve low oil uptake.

Raw material needs - balance and optimisation

Flour, as the most important single raw material in noodle production, must be of appropriate quality. It should have protein content within the range specified, be milled from sound wheat, be cleanly milled to low ash levels, have low starch damage, fine particle size and produce noodles with good texture, good colour development and colour stability. Flour quality should not be considered alone, but in combination with other ingredients and in light of the processing methods used.

There large differences throughout the Pacific Rim region with respect to ingredient quality requirements, but an understanding of the market segmentation and the processing industries will enable raw material requirements to be met. Raw material suppliers need to establish strong links with processors to be in a position to supply more stringent requirements as markets become more discriminating. With the trend towards bigger manufacturers and national and international companies, raw material suppliers must deliver high quality technical service and innovative products that help to simplify their customer's business or deliver cost savings through formulation or processing optimisation.

References

Anon. (1995) Asian Pacific Food Industry November, 80-84.

Anon. (1997a). Cereals International March April,17-18.

Anon. (1997b.) Milling and Baking News Sept. 30, 26-27.

Azudin, M. N., Lo, V. and Alisauskas, V. (1997). Cereals 97 pp 118-121. RACI Melbourne, Australia.

Baik, B.K. Czuchajowski, X. and Pomeranz, Y. (1994). J. Cereal Sci. 19, 291-296

Bean, M.M., Keagy, P.M., Fullington, J.G., Jones F.T. and Mecham, D.K. (1974). Cereal Chem. 51:416-426.

Edwards, R.A., Ross, A.R., Mares, D.J., Ellison, F.W. and Tomlinson, J.D. (1989). J. Cereal Sci. 10,157-167.

Edwards, N.M., Scanlon, M.G., Kruger J.E. and Dexter, J.E. (1996). Cereal Chem. 73,708-711.

Elbers, I.J.W., Ross, A.S. and Quail, K.J. (1996) Cereals 96 pp 128-131. RACI Melbourne, Australia.

Gore P.J., Miskelly D.M. and Moss H.J. (1988). Proc. 38th Aust. Cereal Chem. Conf. pp 97-102. RACI, Melbourne, Australia.

Huang, S.D. (1996a). China - the world's largest consumer of paste products, pp 301-325 in: J. E. Kruger, R. B. Matsuo and J.W. Dick (Eds.) "Pasta and Noodle Technology". AACC, St Paul, MN USA.

Huang, S.D. (1996b). Cereal Foods World, 41,199-204.

Kotwal, Z., Osborne, B.G. Moss, R., McCorquodale, J. Ross, A.S., Bunn, J. and Cracknell, R. L. (1997). Cereals 97 pp 57-61. RACI Melbourne, Australia.

Kim, S.-K. (1996) Instant noodles, pp 195-226 in: J. E. Kruger, R. B. Matsuo and J.W. Dick (Eds.) "Pasta and Noodle Technology". AACC, St Paul, MN USA.

Kim, S.-K. (1997). Cereals 97 pp 96-99. RACI Melbourne, Australia.

Konik, C., Mikkelsen, L.M., Moss. R. and Gore, P.J. (1994). Starch 46, 292-299.

Kruger, J. E. Matsuo, R.R. and Preston, K. (1992). Can. J. Plant Sci. 72, 1021-1029.

Kruger, J.E., Anderson, M.H. and Dexter, J.E. (1994). Cereal Chem. 71, 177-182.

Kun, T. Y. and Basiron, Y. (1994) Palm Oil Developments 21, 19-23.

Lee, C-H., Gore, P.J., Lee, H-D., Yoo B-S. and Hong, S-H. (1987). J. Cereal Sci. 6, 283-297.

Mares, D. (1991). Cereals International pp 41-418. RACI Melbourne, Australia.

Mares, D.J. and Wang, Y. (1995). Cereals 95 pp 380-382. RACI

Melbourne, Australia.

McCallum, J. A. and Walker, J.R.L. (1990). J. Cereal Sci. 12:93-96.

Miskelly, D.M. (1984). J. Sci. Food Agric. 35, 463-471.

Miskelly, D.M. and Moss, H.J. (1985). J. Cereal Sci. 3:379-387.

Miskelly, D. M..(1996) The use of alkali for noodle processing, pp 227-274 in: J. E. Kruger, R. B. Matsuo and J.W. Dick (Eds.) "Pasta and Noodle Technology". AACC, St Paul, MN USA.

Moss, H.J. (1980). Cereal Res. Comm. 8, 297-302.

Moss, H.J. (1985). Chinese noodle production - wheat flour quality and processing factors. Australian Wheat Board, Melbourne, Australia.

Moss, H.J., Miskelly, D.M. and Moss, R. (1986). J. Cereal Sci. 4,261-268.

Moss, R., Gore, P.J. and Murray, I.C. (1987). Food Microstructure 6, 63-74.

Nagao, S.(1996). Processing technology of noodle products in Japan, pp 169-194 in: J. E. Kruger, R. B. Matsuo and J.W. Dick (Eds.) "Pasta and Noodle Technology". AACC, St Paul, MN USA.

Ng A. (1996). Asia Pacific Food Industry December, 58-63.

Oda, M.Y., Yasuda, Y. Okazaki, S., Yamauchi, Y. and Yokoyama, Y. (1980) Cereal Chem. 57,253-254.

Oh, N.H., Seib, P.A., Ward, A. B. and Deyoe, C.W. (1985). Cereal Chem. 62, 441-446.

Park, W.J., Shelton, D.R., Peterson, T.J., Martin, T.J., Kachman, S.D. and Wehling, R.L. (1997). Cereal Chem. 74, 7-11.

Rho K. L., Seib P. A., Chung O. K., Chung D. S. (1986). J. Am. Oil Chem. Soc. 63, 251-256.

Ross, A.S., Quail, K.J. and Crosbie, G.B. (1997). Cereal Chem. 74, 814-820.

Seneur, B. Asp A., and Kinsey, J. (1991). Food trends and the changing consumer, pp 1-12. Eagan Press, St Paul, MN USA.

Shelke K., Dick, J.W., Holm, Y.F. and Loo, K.S. (1990). Cereal Chem. 67,338-342.

Stevens D. G. (1997). World Grain Changing attitudes on wheat quality August 24-29.

Breads of the Pacific Region

S. Huang and K. R. Preston
BRI Australia Limited, North Ryde, NSW, Australia and Grain Research Laboratory, Canadian Grain Commission, Winnipeg, Manitoba, Canada

Introduction

The Pacific region extends from the southern tip of South America, north through North America then south again through northern Asia, south east Asia, Australia and New Zealand. Throughout this region, bread consumption and preference varies widely. South American, Central American and Mexican consumers consume wheat primarily in the form of hearth breads while North American consumers in the United States and Canada as well as those in Australia and New Zealand consume wheat primarily in the form of pan bread. In these regions wheat is also generally the primarily cereal grain consumed and thus consumption of these products is high on a per capita basis. However maize and, to a lesser extent, rice and manioc are also important in many South and Central American countries as well as Mexico. In Pacific Rim countries of Asia, wheat is primarily consumed in the form of noodles and steamed bread. Bread consumption probably averages about 15-30% of wheat flour usage. In China, steamed bread represents the most popular wheaten food and is major form of bread eaten. Pan breads and, to a lesser extent, steamed bread, are most popular in the remainder of this region. The only exception is the Philippines where hearth bread represents a high proportion of wheat flour consumption. In this paper, the three major bread types consumed in the Pacific rim region are discussed.

Hearth Breads

Hearth breads represent the main form of wheat consumption in Pacific Rim countries of South America, Central America, Mexico and the Philippines. This preference is likely a reflection of the mainly Spanish (and other southern European) influence in these countries. With the exception of the Philippines, hearth bread probably represents over 80% of total bread consumption with pan breads at less than 10%. In the Philippines, hearth bread represents about 50% of bread consumption, pan breads account for about 30% and other bread types including buns and sweet bread account for the remainder (N. Uy, personal communication). In the remainder of the Pacific Rim, hearth breads (primarily French-type) are considered as specialty breads and represent a relatively low percentage of overall bread consumption relative to pan breads in most countries and steamed buns in Asian countries. However, in North America, Australia and New Zealand, these breads are growing in popularity and represent a significant percentage of specialty bread production, particularly in urban areas. In the United States, hearth bread represents about 12% of overall bread production (Faridi and Faubion, 1995). In most Asian countries, hearth breads are not popular due to consumers' aversion to crusty products. Nonetheless, hearth bread consumption is growing in this region, particularly in Japan, and particularly among younger consumers.

The types of hearth breads preferred in countries of the Pacific Rim vary widely in shape, size, formulation and processing conditions. In general, consumers in all of the major hearth bread consuming markets except Colombia prefer smaller (bun) sized products. Lean formulas are generally used in Chile, Peru, Bolivia, Mexico and the Philippines while rich (high fat and sugar) formulas are preferred in Colombia and Ecuador. In Central America, both rich and lean formulas are common, with the relative amount of each type dependent on the country and the region (rural or urban) (Peña, 1995). For most of these countries, one bread type usually predominates, particularly in rural areas. With increasing urbanisation and a growing middle class, the choice of products is becoming wider due to consumer demand. In many of the cities, various French-type hearth breads, other hearth breads, white pan breads and soft buns are increasing at the expense of traditional breads. Deregulation of the wheat and flour industry in most South American countries has accelerated this process by making available a wider range of flour types at market driven prices. However, deregulation has also resulted in reduced government subsidisation and/or control of flour and/or bread prices in some countries which has increased bread prices and reduced consumption. Although the vast majority of bread is still produced in small bakeries, there is also a trend to medium and larger sized bakeries which can produce a wider range of products more efficiently. The major constraint to the proliferation of these bakeries is the strong consumer preference for very fresh bread.

1. Lean Formula Hearth Breads Markets

Chile has the second highest per capita common wheat consumption in the western hemisphere at about 90 kg/year (David, 1997). The major bread consumed in this market is maraquetta, a lean formula hearth bread bun. A medium strong, straight grade flour with an ash level of about 0.58% is widely used. For upscale bakeries, a lower ash, strong flour with an ash of about 0.50% is preferred. Flour protein content varies (9 - 12%) but values of 11% or more are preferred. Maraquetta bun formulation and processing conditions vary. Formulations include flour (100%), salt (1.8 - 2.0%), yeast (up to 3%), water (60% or less) and improver which may contain oxidant (AA or bromate), surfactant (normally SSL) and amylase (normally fungal). Fat and sugar are sometimes added at low levels. A straight dough procedure is used for preparing these buns involving mixing of ingredients, fermentation, make-up (normally by hand), proofing (variable) and baking. In upscale bakeries, higher speed mixers (spiral) are sometimes used to develop the dough , reducing fermentation requirements. Higher yeast levels are also used which reduces proof times to about 30 min. For most bakeries, a low speed mixer is used to mix ingredients and dough development is completed using longer fermentation. It is also common in some areas to develop the dough by sheeting (dough break) after fermentation. Longer fermentation also reduces the levels of yeast required but necessitates longer proof time to get sufficient dough rise before baking. The longer proof time (up to several hours or more) has advantages to the baker since he can bake fresh bread from the same batch over an extended period of time as needed. "Mother sponges" and "old dough" are sometimes used to enhance flavour and reduce yeast requirements.

Hand make-up is the key to obtaining the characteristic shape of maraquetta buns. Dough pieces of about 100 g are rounded and slightly flattened. Two pieces are then joined together (side by side), put on cloth and indented longitudinally using a wooden dowel, inverted to reduce skinning, rested, inverted again, and then given a final proof prior to baking. The indentations formed by joining the pieces and the indentation longitudinally result in a cross being evident on the final product.

In Peru, tolette buns are most popular. They share similarities to maraquetta buns from Chile and flautas from Argentina. A lean formula containing strong flour, salt (about 1.5%), sugar (1%, variable), yeast (usually less than 1%) and water (<60%) is used. Until recently, bread improvers have not been widely used. Small amounts of fat may sometimes also be added (<1%). Most tolette buns are produced by a straight dough procedure which features dough development by dough brake after fermentation. Fermentation times can vary widely (1-6 hr) depending on yeast level, flour quality and initial mixing conditions (hand mixing, slow speed mixing or less commonly, higher speed mixing). Final proof time can also vary widely, ranging from 1 hr to 12 hr with longer times most common. Longer proof times (using less yeast) allow bakers to produce fresh bread from the same dough batch over a long time period. Make-up is by hand. Tolette buns are usually produced from 35 g dough pieces which are rounded, shaped, compressed longitudinally, indented longitudinally (usually with a wood dowel), inverted to prevent skinning, rested, inverted again and proofed prior to baking. The final product has an extended shape with an indentation in the middle running the length of the bun.

Per capita consumption of wheat in Bolivia is about 53 kg per year (David, 1997). Most bread is produced in small bakeries with maraquetta buns being the most prominent product. This 30-40 g hearth bun is produced from straight grade flour (normally 77 to 78% extraction, about 0.55% ash, as is basis) using medium strength and strong imported wheat of about 11-12% protein. A typical formulation includes flour (100%), yeast (1.5%), salt (1.5%), and water (64%). Small amounts of sugar, fat and ascorbic acid are sometimes added. Maraquetta buns are usually mixed by hand or slow speed mixing followed by a long fermentation (4-6 hr) in a trough. Dough is then divided into 40 g pieces, rounded, rested, shaped, rested, cut, proofed (0.5-1 hr) and baked. All "handling" operations are usually done by hand. Dough is not put through sheeting rolls during make-up. Dough breaks are sometimes used to develop the dough after fermentation. The product has a very high specific volume (up to 10 cc/g) and a very open texture (due to lack of sheeting). Since Bolivia is located at very high altitudes (4000m) in the Andes, the low atmospheric pressure has a significant impact on baking. This factor contributes to high specific volume by enhancing oven spring. The high water absorption is also a reflection of high water loss during baking.

In Mexico, wheat consumption is approximately 33 kg/person per year. Most bread is produced in small bakeries with bolillo (Figure 1) being the most common (40-50% of bread production). A typical formulation for bolillo is flour (medium strength, 10-11% protein, 0.54% ash, as is basis), 1.6% sugar, 2.0% salt, 55-60% water and improver containing ascorbic acid (sometimes with DATEM, soybean flour and monoglycerides). The use of "mother sponge" (about 15% of total dough weight) is common to improve flavour and dough strength. Processing conditions can vary but most bolillo is prepared using a straight dough procedure. Ingredients are mixed in slow speed mixers (spiral mixers used in upscale bakeries), fermented for varying periods of time, scaled (80-90g), rested, shaped, proofed and cut longitudinally then baked. With slow speed mixers, it is not uncommon to develop dough after fermentation using a dough brake.

Figure 1. Bolillo hearth bread from Mexico.

Pan de sal, a small hearth bread roll, is the most common bread produced in the Philippines (Nagao, 1995). In contrast to the products described above, this hearth bread is produced from straight grade (about 0.56% ash, as is basis) higher protein (12.5 to 13.5%) strong wheat flours. Small bakeries predominate, using a long fermentation (about 5 hr) straight dough process, although no-time and sponge and dough processes are also common. After fermentation, dough is further developed using dough brakes which enhances oven spring and leads to the finer crumb structure preferred by consumers. A basic formula for pan de sal includes flour (100%), sugar (6%), salt (1.5%), shortening (4%), instant yeast (1.5%), water (58%) and improver. A richer formula containing about 16% sugar and 10% shortening is also popular.

2. Rich Formula Hearth Breads Markets

Wheat consumption in Colombia and Ecuador averages about 29 and 41 kg per person per year, respectively (David, 1997). In both markets, a unique style hearth bread with high fat and sugar content is produced, primarily in small bakeries. These breads have a fine almost cake-like structure and a shinny exterior appearance due to the use of egg wash prior to baking. In Colombia, bakers were motivated to use high levels of fat and sugar which were in excess supply when government regulated flour supplies were insufficient to meet demands (E. Payeras, personnel communication). Consumers became used to these products because of the unique flavour and high energy value. Recent attempts by the government and the milling industry to promote leaner formulations due to health concerns and excess milling capacity have been less than successful.

In Colombia, aliñado bread (Figure 2) is the major bread product consumed. This bread normally weighs about 500 g. Smaller buns are also common using similar formulations and processing conditions. A medium strong to strong straight grade flour (approximately 0.58% ash, as is basis) with a protein content of about 10.5 to 11.5 % is used although there is a trend towards the use of higher protein, stronger flour. The higher ash is partially the result of mills removing a portion of low ash reduction flour for pasta production. Formulations for aliñado bread vary widely in terms of fat and sugar content. Sugar ranges from 4 to 12% or higher with the upper figure more common in the Cali area. Fat content normally varies from 10 to 25%. Other ingredients include salt (about 2%), yeast (2.5 to 4%), water (45 to

50%) and eggs (up to 13%). The higher yeast level is a reflection of reduced activity due to the impact of the sugar and fat. Lower water absorption is also due to high fat level as well as the use of dough breaks and the required product properties. A straight dough process is normally used. Dough is mixed by hand or in low speed mixers then rested, scaled, developed using dough brakes, rested, hand rounded and shaped, slashed (3 cross cuts), proofed for 45 to 60 min and baked. An egg wash is used to give the product a glaze. Dough is scaled starting after about 20 min of fermentation and, with larger dough, is completed after about 60 min. The dough is scaled after fermentation to accommodate the smaller capacity of the dough brake. Details of a laboratory scale aliñado bread procedure have been published (Dexter *et al*, 1989, 1990).

Figure 2. Aliñado bread from Colombia

In Ecuador, smaller hearth buns dominate the market using formulation and processing conditions similar to those used in Colombia. In both countries, lean formula hearth breads are becoming more popular at the expense of the traditional bread in urban middle class areas. Pan breads produced in recently opened larger bakeries are also gaining in popularity.

Pan Breads

Pan breads, including white breads, variety breads (brown, whole wheat, multi-grain, fruit and related breads) and soft buns (hamburger, hot dog and related buns) are the major form of wheat consumption in Canada, United States, Australia and New Zealand. In the United States per capita consumption of white, variety and soft buns is approximately 12.8, 5.8 and 6.0 kg per year (Faridi and Faubion, 1995). Canadian figures are similar. In Australia and New Zealand, approximately 60 % of flour used for human consumption is used to produce bread. White sliced bread predominates in these markets but variety breads are also important (McMaster and Gould, 1995).

Most pan breads in these countries are produced in industrial bakeries. In Australia and New Zealand, large bakeries account for approximately 65 and 80% of bread production, respectively. In-store bakeries, located in supermarkets, and hot bread shops are growing in popularity and account for most of the remainder (McMaster and Gould, 1995). In the United States and Canada, industrial bakeries probably account for 50-60% of bread production. The proliferation of in-store bakeries over the last 20 years has also made them a major force in the market, particularly for variety breads. Small bakeries, many of which produce specialty breads for distribution, are a small but important contributor to overall pan bread production. In Canada in 1995 there were 454 wholesale bakery plants and over 3000 retail in-store and small local bakeries (Statistics Canada, 1996). This can be compared to the approximately 300 in-store bakeries in Australia (with approximately 2/3 of Canada's population) where this production base is still evolving (McMaster and Gould, 1995).

Pan bread formulations and processing conditions (Table 1) vary among the four "western" countries discussed above. Table 1 gives details for the most common process(es) in these countries (Yamada and Preston, 1992, Faridi and Faubion, 1995 McMaster and Gould, 1995, B. Hogan, personal communication, N. Larsen and A. Wilson, personal communication). In the United Stated, sponge and dough is the predominant process accounting for about 61% of total bread production (Faridi and Faubion, 1995). Straight dough processing is used widely in in-store and small bakeries and, in general, for specialty bread production. Strong straight grade flour with a protein content of about 11.2 to 11.7% and 0.44-0.46% ash (14.0% mb) is normally used. In Canada, the no-time dough (Canadian short) process is most widely used although sponge and dough processing is still popular in eastern Canada and straight dough is used widely in in-store and small bakeries, particularly for specialty breads. Bakers flour in Canada is normally produced from split stream milling where some of the low ash reduction flour is removed for other (home use, etc.) purposes and additional early and middle break flour is added. Flour ash is normally about 0.55% (14% mb) and protein is about 12.0-12.5%. In both the United States and Canada, large bar mixers are used in bread factories to develop dough. Many Canadian bakeries run their bar mixers at higher speeds compared to their southern neighbours due to the lack of fermentation which results in higher mixing requirements for proper dough development. In-store and smaller bakeries use a wide range of mixers with spiral types becoming increasingly popular due to their high mixing efficiency. In-store bakeries also make extensive use of frozen dough to reduce processing space requirements and to offer a wider range of products. In contrast to Europe, par-baked products are not widely used.

As shown in Table 1, American formulations are much sweeter than the other three countries. Both fat and sugar levels are lowest in Australian and New Zealand formulations. Baking absorption is highest in Canada. This may be partly due to the higher protein flours used by Canadian baking plants. Canadian mills also produce higher starch damage flours for no-time baking processes which contribute to higher absorption. Bromate and ascorbic acid are common oxidants used in the United States but the former is banned in the other three countries. In Canada, ADA and ascorbic acid as well as enzymes have been used to replace bromate while in Australia and New Zealand, ascorbic acid is the major additive used for oxidation.

Table 1. Typical formulations and processing conditions used in United States, Canada, Australia and New Zealand to produce white sandwich bread.

Ingredient[1]	United States		Canada		Australia	New Zealand
	Sponge & Dough[2]		Straight[3]	No-time[4]	No-time[5]	No-time[5]
	Sponge (%)	Dough (%)	Dough (%)	Dough (%)	Dough (%)	Dough (%)
Flour	70	30	100	100	100	100
Yeast	3.0	-	2.5	3.0	2.5	3.0
Salt	-	2.0	2.0	2.4	2.0	2.0
Sugar	-	8.5	8.0	4.0	1.0	0.0
Shortening	-	3.0	2.75	3.0	2.0	2.0
NFDM	-	2.0	2.0	4.0	4.0	
Water	40	24	64	70	58	60-62

[1] Figures relate to compressed yeast. Sugar is sometimes replaced by sweetener solids. Non-fat dry milk (NFDM) is sometimes replaced by whey. Improvers such as yeast food, vinegar, mono- and di-glycerides, dough strengtheners and calcium proprionate are normally added. Commonly used oxidants in the United States include bromate and ascorbic acid. Bromate is banned in the other three countries and ascorbic acid is used. ADA is also used in Canada.

[2] Sponges are mixed for several min then fermented for 3-5 hr at 30°C. Dough ingredients are added and mixed to optimum (1 min slow then 10-12 min at high speed in a bar mixer). Dough is divided, rounded, rested (about 7 min), sheeted, shaped and panned. After a 55 min proof at 42°C (85% rh), dough is baked at 230°C for about 18 min.

[3] Dough ingredients are mixed 1 min at low speed and 15-20 min at high speed then fermented about 2 hr at 30-35°C. Dough is then treated as described for the sponge and dough process.

[4] Dough ingredients are mixed at high speed in a bar mixer for about 10-15 min (< 30°C), divided and rounded, rested for 2-5 min, sheeted and moulded, proofed at 35-40°C for about 50 min then baked at 230°C for about 20 min.

[5] Processing conditions are similar in Australia and New Zealand as described for Canada above ([4]). Australian bread plants use both high speed

bar mixers and Chorleywood type very high speed mixers while in New Zealand, the latter type of mixer is predominant.

Australian and New Zealand bakery plants use no-time dough processing conditions. In Australia, both high speed bar and very high speed "Chorleywood" type mixers are used widely, while in New Zealand, "Chorleywood" type mixers predominate. In New Zealand, mixing times are varied depending on the requirements of the flour (normally about 3 min at about 12 wh/kg total energy input). Delayed vacuum (about 0.5 atm) is normally applied after 50-75% of work input (N. Larsen and A. Wilson, personnel communication). The delay in applying vacuum promotes oxidation by allowing activation of ascorbic acid. Australian bakery flours vary in protein content from 10.5% in southern states to 12.5% in northern states while New Zealand bakery flours have a protein content of about 10.5%. Both countries use colour grade (Kent Jones) rather than ash to determine flour refinement. Australian bakery flours vary from 0 to 2 KJ units while New Zealand flours have colour grade values less than 1.5 KJ units.

Pan breads in the Asian Pacific rim region are considered as both specialty and premium products. With the exception of China and the Philippines, approximately 15-30% of wheat flour production is used for pan bread production (Nagao, 1995). In general, consumers in this region prefer a soft bland tasting product where crumb mouth feel characteristics are highly important. This preference is the major reason why white pan breads predominate. Very little variety bread is consumed in these markets due to the harsher crumb and stronger taste associated with these products. The taste and texture of the crust is generally not popular with consumers. Crust is often removed from white pan bread and the remaining crumb slices are wrapped for sale More recently, soft buns have grown in popularity and the market for a wider range of bread products such as French type and variety breads has been increasing, particularly in Japan. This change is being primarily driven by younger consumers who are developing more "western" tastes. Baking companies are also actively introducing new products to increase both overall bread consumption and their market share.

In the northern Asian region (South Korea, Japan and Taiwan), industrial pan bread is usually producing by the sponge and dough method. Smaller bakeries normally use straight dough processing procedures. The quality of bread produced is generally very high. The most popular product is square pan bread with a very white fine crumb. In Japan, square pan bread accounts for about 55% of overall bread production (Nagao, 1995). The crumb has a very tender , fine and moist texture preferred by Japanese consumers. This bread is normally produced from strong very low ash (<0.40%) ash flour with a protein content of 12.0 to 12.5%. Details of formulation and processing conditions have been previously published (Yamada and Preston, 1994). In Taiwan and South Korea, similar flours with higher ash content are used.

In south east Asia, open top bread produced in medium to small sized bakeries predominates. In Malaysia and Thailand, high protein (about 14.0%) strong flours are used in bread production. A straight dough procedure is commonly used where dough is developed after fermentation using dough breaks. As in South America, this method of developing dough results in a very fine white crumb structure with high volume potential. Specific volumes (volume/weight) of some of this type of bread can be as high as 12 cc/g. However, the use of dough breaks is labour intensive, requires strong high protein flours and limits production capacity. There is a growing tendency to use higher speed mixers including "Chorleywood" type processes to increase production and lower costs

Steamed Bread

Steamed bread has its origin in China where it has been consumed in its various forms for more than 1700 years. Over the centuries, probably as a result of trade between countries in the region, steamed bread spread from China to Japan, Korea and south-east Asian countries. Today, steamed bread represents around 70% of the end usage of flour in northern China (Huang and Miskelly, 1991) and 30-40% in southern China. Over 1.3 billion people consume steamed bread and buns regularly in this region. The commercial production of frozen steamed bread, buns and twisted rolls has raised their popularity even further.

Steamed bread is a leavened wheat flour product, which is cooked by steaming in a steamer. The most common type of steamed breads, weighing about 130 - 150g, are either round or roughly cylindrical in shape, white in colour and have a smooth, shiny surface devoid of a crust. The texture varies from dense to open and the flavour varies to suit local tastes (Huang *et al.*, 1991). Like pan bread, one piece of steamed bread dough can be made into different types of products. Steamed bread can be made with or without fillings. The products without filling are called steamed bread (*mantou or mo)* (Figure 3) and with fillings called steamed buns (*baozi* or *bao*) (Figure 4). The common fillings for steamed buns are meats, vegetables and sweet red bean or lotus bean pastes. Other forms of steamed bread include twisted rolls with various shapes (*huajuan*) (Figure 5).

Figure 3. Steamed bread (*mantou*) of different shapes and sizes.

1. Steamed bread (mantou)

Three main styles of steamed bread have been recognised in China and east and south east Asian countries, viz., northern, southern and Guangdong styles (Huang *et al.*, 1995). The differences in quality preference,

Figure 4. Steamed buns *(bao* or *baozi)* with different fillings
(Reprinted, with permission from Technomic Publishing Co., Inc.).

Figure 5. Steamed rolls with different shapes *(huajuan)*
(Reprinted, with permission from Technomic Publishing Co., Inc.).

ingredients and consumption regions among the three styles of steamed bread are listed in Table 2. The northern style (so-called *changmian mantou*), which is preferred in northern China, has a very cohesive and elastic eating quality, a higher arch-domed shape and a dense structure. The southern style (so called *xiaomian mantou*, derived in southern China), now widely popular throughout China, has a soft, elastic and medium cohesive eating quality, a lower arch-domed shape and an open structure. Guangdong style steamed bread, which is popular in the very southern part of China (i.e. Guangdong, Fujian, Hainan, Taiwan and Hong Kong) and east and south east Asian countries, has an open structure, a sweet taste and a very soft and elastic, but not cohesive eating quality. Steamed buns are the most popular product for this style steamed bread. People usually have this style of steamed buns as a snack.

Steamed bread is a staple food in the wheat growing area of northern China. In contrast, rice and noodles are more popular in the south, where people often consume steamed bread for breakfast. Steamed buns with a variety of fillings are popular throughout China.

Steamed bread dough for northern and southern style steamed bread is made of flour, water and sour dough with no sugar, fat or salt added. In Guangdong style steamed bread, up to 25% of sugar, 10% of fat and 1.2% of salt are added.

Table 2. The main differences of three styles of steamed bread

	Northern	Southern	Guangdong
Fat(%)	0	0	up to 10%
Sugar(%)	0	0	up to 25%
SV*	~ 2.5	~ 3.0	~ 2.8 - 3.2
Structure	Dense	Open	Open
Eating quality	Elastic, very Cohesive	soft, elastic and Cohesive	very soft and elastic but not cohesive
Popular area	Northern China	all China	very southern China and south-east Asia

* SV = specific volume

A. Preparation

In China most steamed bread is fermented using either freshly prepared 'starter' dough or sour dough kept from the previous day. Sour dough is cheap and readily available.

When sour dough fermentation is used, the fermented dough is very sour due to fermentation by-products of the *Lactobacillus* spp. Fully fermented 'starter' dough is suitable for steamed bread making, whereas over-fermented or old 'starter' dough is not. Baking powder is occasionally used for steamed bread made at home.

The 'sponge and dough process' is a traditional procedure for steamed bread making, The traditional stages included in making steamed bread are as follows (Huang *et al.*, 1991): mixing of dough, fermentation, neutralisation, re-mixing, moulding, proofing and steaming.

Mixing of Dough

Dough is traditionally mixed by hand in the home. In steamed bread making, the dough mixing process has two main objectives: (a) the thorough and uniform dispersion of ingredients to form a homogeneous mixture and (b) to bring about the physical development of gluten in the dough into a uniform structure. Such a structure possesses an optimum degree of plasticity, elasticity and viscous flow. In the traditional sponge and dough process, the first of these objectives is attained during mixing. The physical development of gluten in the dough is achieved by the mixing, re-mixing and fermentation processes. These operations result in a continuous three-dimensional network of thin, hydrated protein films that enclose the starch granules and flour particles together with occluded air bubbles.

Fermentation

Proper dough fermentation is very important for the production of steamed bread. Different styles of steamed bread require different fermentation time. When 'starter' dough is used, fermentation of steamed bread dough includes

158

three steps: the preparation of 'starter' dough, dough fermentation and neutralisation.

The 'starter' dough is prepared freshly by dispersing the sour dough remaining at the end of the day into water, adding additional flour, and allowing the dough to ferment overnight for use on the following day.

There are four types of fermentation process, which are used for different types of steamed bread.

Full fermentation (1 - 3 hours, depending on the season) is used to make dough for steamed bread of southern style, steamed rolls and steamed buns (*da bao*).

Partial fermentation (0.5 - 1.5 hours) is used to make dough suitable for steamed buns with juicy fillings (*xiao bao*).

No - time fermentation is increasingly used in commercial production of steamed bread. Flour, water, starter dough and sodium carbonate are mixed, and the dough is then moulded, proofed and steamed. The amount of sodium carbonate added is variable (about 6g per kg of flour) and depends on both the temperature in proofing cabinet and proof time.

Re-mixed fermentation dough is often used to make northern style steamed bread. After the dough is fully fermented, more flour is mixed in at a ratio of additional flour to fermented dough up to 40% by weight. Another use for this dough is for making a type of steamed bread with a cross cut on the top surface (*kaihua mantou*) (Huang *et al.*, 1991).

Neutralisation and Re-mixing

As the full fermented dough is acidic, it needs to be neutralised with an alkali such as a 40% sodium carbonate solution. It is critical to control this stage for good quality steamed bread. If the dough is over-neutralised, the steamed bread will become yellow or dark in colour with a strong alkaline flavour and an objectionable bitter taste due to hydrolysis of protein to small peptides. Steamed bread made from under-neutralised dough has a sour smell and taste, smaller volume, poor appearance and dense structure. The pH of dough before neutralisation is 3.7 - 4.0, and after neutralisation is 6.4 - 6.7 (Huang *et al.*, 1991).

Addition of alkali assists fermentation as it neutralises acids produced by lactic acid bacteria during fermentation and allows the production of carbon dioxide and water by yeast. However, it does destroy some vitamins in the dough. The amount of alkali required varies with the extent of fermentation, temperature and ambient conditions. Experience is required both in judging the correct level of alkali and in the technique of alkali addition.

Several sensory methods are used to check the degree of neutralisation. These include the smell, taste and structure of the cut dough section, the sound made on striking the dough with the palm of the hand, or cooking a test piece of dough (Anon, 1989). The neutralisation point can also be determined by checking the pH of the dough.

The neutralisation process can be carried out either by hand or by a mechanical mixer. When the neutralisation is complete, the dough may require further mixing depending on the strength of the flour used and the style of steamed bread to be made.

Moulding

The dough is divided into pieces, usually weighing 130 - 150g. The dough can be moulded into a long cylindrical piece and cut into smaller pieces or shaped into round domes either by hand or by a moulding machine.

Proofing

Dough pieces are placed on a tray usually made of bamboo or. In the home, proofing is carried out at room temperature. In factories proofing is carried out in a proofing cabinet, where temperature and humidity are controlled, for 40 - 50 minutes at about $40^{\circ}C$ when the 'no time dough' procedure is used.

Steaming

The tray containing the dough pieces is transferred to a steamer and is steamed for about 20 minutes with the appropriate steaming rate. Optimum steaming has been achieved if the bread recovers to its original state after the surface of the steamed bread is gently pressed with the index finger.

B. Serving

Steamed bread is usually served when it is hot. In northern China when people have their meals, hot steamed bread is consumed as an accompaniment to the cooked dishes rather than in the sandwich form which may be more familiar to westerners. In southern China hot steamed bread and rice porridge served with some preserved vegetables are a popular traditional breakfast.

2. Steamed Buns (*baozi*)

There are numerous varieties of steamed buns with differences in sizes, textures, shapes and fillings. Despite this wide range, there are really two major types of steamed buns: *da bao* (big buns) (50g of flour for one or two buns) and *xiao bao* (small buns) (50g of flour for 3-5 pieces of steamed buns). The dough for *da bao* is fully fermented, while the dough for *xiao bao* is partially fermented, typically using half or one third of the time required for full fermentation. The partially fermented dough is soft and tender, yet still has the strength to hold the juicy fillings. The texture of *da bao* is open and of *xiao bao* is dense. The range of fillings is diverse (sweet and savoury) for *da bao* and usually only juicy savoury filling (adding chicken or pork broth) is used for *xiao bao* (keeping the filling in a refrigerator for 1-2 hours can make it firmer for use). Meanwhile, *xiao bao* is more delicate in shape and filling and it is served immediately after steaming in small steamer (Huang *et al* 1994).

There are two types of fillings for steamed buns: sweet and savoury.

Sweet fillings include sugar, cooked beans, red bean paste, lotus bean paste, red (or black) jujube date, chopped leaf lard mixed with sugar, mixture of various nuts with sugar. Other common sweet fillings include sesame seed, dried fruits, preserved mixture of Chinese wisteria flower, preserved mixture of rose flower and sugar, taro paste.

Savoury fillings include chopped vegetables (raw or cooked), various meats and sea food (prawn and crab meat) or a combination of both. To make the filling moist and tender, raw minced meat is often mixed with seasoning and water (popular in northern China) or gel solution made of finely chopped cooked pork skin (popular in southern China).

A. Preparation

Making the buns

Steamed buns are usually made from southern style and Guangdong style dough. Steamed buns made from southern style dough are popular in all of China except the lower region of southern China. The steamed buns made from Guangdong style dough are popular in the lower region of southern China, i.e., Guangdong, Fujian, Hainan, Taiwan and Hong Kong and east and south east Asian countries The fermented dough (described above) is transferred to a lightly floured work surface and kneaded a few times. It is hand rolled into a cylinder 40 cm long and 4 cm wide. The cylinder is cut into 2.5 cm pieces. The pieces are turned on their flat ends and pressed with the palm to flatten. Each piece is rolled into a 7.5 cm circular shaped piece, rotating the dough around and rolling the edges thinner than the centre.

About 1.5 tablespoons filling is placed in the centre of the round flattened dough. The filling is sealed within the dough by pinching and pleating the edges of the round dough together. In China and other east and south east Asian countries, buns with sweet filling are typically steamed upside down to identify them as sweet ones. After steaming, these sweet buns may be identified with a spot of red food colouring (Lin, 1986).

Proofing and Steaming

Each filled bun is placed on a 7.5 cm square of non-stick baking paper and then placed spaced apart on a baking sheet. They are left in a warm place for about 20 - 30 min (depending on temperature), or until they almost double in size. The buns (on the paper) are then transferred to the steamer rack, placed about 2.5 cm apart. The buns are steamed over medium heat for 15 to 20 min.

B. Serving

The best way to serve the buns is directly from steamer, otherwise they can be cooled and later reheated. They are usually served as a snack or for lunch and are very popular with tourists and business people.

3. Steamed Rolls (*huajuan*)

Steamed rolls (*huajuan*) are another common type of steamed product. Within this category there are a variety of shapes and flavours. Steamed rolls have the following method of preparation in common. Fermented and neutralised dough is rolled out into a large thin, flat (may be round, square or rectangular) shape. A layer of a particular condiment is spread over this dough which is then rolled and cut into pieces, twisted or shaped and then steamed. In general steamed rolls can be divided into three groups: rolled rolls, folded rolls and stretched rolls.

Rolled Rolls (*juan huajuan*)

The fully fermented dough for southern or Guangdong style steamed bread is neutralised and kneaded until it is smooth. The dough is rolled into thin rectangular pieces of even thickness. It is brushed with vegetable oil and sprinkled with salt and flour (or fillings such as sugar, sweet bean paste, jujube date, sesame paste, chopped shallots, five-spice powder, Sichuan peppercorn powder or other savoury fillings). The dough is rolled tightly from one end to the other (or from both sides towards the middle) to form a long cylinder. The cylinder is cut into small pieces (about 35 or 70g of dough) and formed into different shapes, proofed and steamed for about 20 min. The variety of fillings and shapes make these types of rolls very attractive.

Folded Rolls (*zhedie juan*)

A well-known variety is "One thousand layer" rolls. The processing procedure is as follows. The fully fermented dough is neutralised and kneaded until smooth. The dough is rolled into a 27 cm square piece and cut down the centre into two equal pieces. One piece is brushed with vegetable oil and sprinkled with flour and the other piece is placed on top. This process is repeated until the dough piece has 2, 4, 8, 16 and 32 layers after folding 5 times. Finally the dough piece is rolled into a 4 cm thick cylinder, proofed and steamed. The product is cut into 5 cm thick pieces and served. (Anon, 1989).

Stretched Rolls (*chen huajuan*)

These types of rolls are made from sheets of stretched dough. Two popular varieties are "Silver thread" rolls and "Golden thread" rolls.

To make the "silver thread", the oiled and stretched dough string is cut into 16 cm long pieces. Twenty five of the cut pieces are combined together and holding each end of the combined strings with each hand, they are twisted and folded back on themselves. The formed dough is proofed, steamed and served.

Commercial production

Traditionally, steamed bread is made at home. Most women in rural northern China know how to make beautiful steamed bread. In the past two decades, the fast growing economies in China, East and south east Asian countries have led to an improvement of living standards. More and more people prefer the convenience of commercially manufactured steamed bread. Thus, there is an increasing trend for production in small factories or workshops. A great number of such workshops can be found in the cities of northern China.

Steamed bread, buns and rolls manufactured by small factories or individual enterprises are often sold on the street or in busy places in the morning to people on their way to work , or at lunch time. People in cities buy steamed bread from the market and reheat the bread before meals.

Most steamed bread factories are simply equipped, with a slow speed mixer and a machine for moulding. Much of these steamed bread factories are still heavily dependent on manual labour.

Several big ycast manufacturers have been established in recent years in China. The use of yeast in the fermentation of steamed bread dough has greatly been increased. More and more commercial steamed bread factories use a 'no time dough process'. Therefore southern style steamed bread is more popular than ever before in whole China.

There is increasing production of steamed bread, buns and rolls in factories equipped with more advanced machines. An automatic production line for steamed bread was established in China in 1980's (Huang *et al.*, 1994).

In China a type of moulding machine has been widely used for nearly ten years. It consists of a hopper, feed assembly, and shaping rolls, which develops gluten similar to by dough sheeting (Chen, 1992). In the moulding process, dough is pushed by the plucking blade in the hopper and conveyed into conical part of the feed screw. The dough is then compressed gradually. The dough is pushed into the forming assembly and cut into pieces by the blades there. The dough pieces move through two rotating rolls, which mould them into a smooth, round shape. The dough balls then fall through a chute and are then proofed and steamed. There are several factories in China which produce moulding machines and the quality and reliability of them tends to vary.

Recently, a medium sized steamed bread production line was built in Beijing with 15,000 kg per day production capacity. In other regions and countries such as Hong Kong, Taiwan, Japan, Korea and some south east Asian countries, more advanced machinery is used to produce steamed buns and steamed bread.

Encrusters can be used to produce steamed buns (with fillings). The encruster gradually squeezes the dough out by two screws. When the dough reaches the compound nozzle, it is formed into a ring or doughnut shape in a continuous strip. Filling is co-extruded inside the casting at the same time. Ends of the strip are then sealed to form a ball mass. The encruster is also capable of mechanically moulding the shape of the buns, to imitate the form of hand made ones.

There are several manufacturers, who produce modern steamed bread and bun machines, such as RHEON (Japan) and YANG ZHENG (Taiwan).

Many innovative products have been developed, particularly among those distributed to supermarket chains. Sold both fresh and frozen, a variety of fillings are available and layered steamed breads with chocolate, coffee, panda or taro colourings have been widely marketed.

Whole meal steamed bread has also recently appeared in market. As well, there are some new types of steamed breads made from mixtures of wheat flour with other flours such as buckwheat, millet, sorghum or maize flour. These new products are marketed as healthy foods and are sold in grain stores in northern China.

There are also some new ways of serving steamed bread. Steamed bread is cut into pieces and sliced cooked meat, ham, chicken, or smoked fish are put between steamed bread pieces and served like sandwiches.

Frozen Products - Convenient Food

Because steamed bread has a very soft and moist surface, it is an ideal medium to support bacterial and fungal growth. Hence the shelf life of steamed bread is short.

Freezing, chilling and microwave technologies have made these traditional foods more convenient for modern life (Figure 6). The freezing process greatly extends the shelf life of these products. Adding to the convenience, frozen products can be re-heated directly in a microwave oven for only about 1 minute. Now people can have hot, delicious steamed buns for breakfast almost as simply as having corn flakes.

There are still a lot of new challenges facing the manufacturer to improve the quality of steamed bread. For example what are the optimum procedures for freezing and microwave reheating processes? More research is needed to resolve some of the adverse effects of freezing and microwave reheating processes on the quality of steamed bread.

Figure 6. Colourfully packed frozen steamed bread, buns and rolls.

Current and Potential Market Status

Fresh and frozen buns are very popular in Japan, Korea, China and south east Asian countries. Currently in China, people in the city still buy more unpacked fresh steamed bread, buns and rolls than the packed chilled and frozen ones simply because of the price. However, as the living standard continues to improve the consumption of packed chilled or frozen steamed bread, buns and rolls will continue to increase steadily.

Acknowledgments

The authors would like to thank Dr. J. Dexter, Grain Research Laboratory, Canadian Grain Commission, and Mr. A. Tweed and Mr. D. Tully, Canadian International Grains Institute for providing information on South American bread markets. We are also very grateful to Mrs Sandi Ormston and Mr. Steven Zounis for their excellent photographic work.

References

Anon, 1989. Techniques to Making Wheaten Foods. Beijing: Chinese Commercial Publishing House (in Chinese).

Anon, 1992. Four Hundred Varieties of Delicious Wheaten Foods. Beijing: Jinn Dun Publishing House (in Chinese).

Cheng, L. M. Food Machinery for the production of Cereal Foods, Snack Foods and Confectionery. Ellis Horrid, New York, 1992.

David, J. 1997. Wheat product use: trends in Latin America, World Grain, August: 6-8.

Dexter, J. E., Kilborn, R. H. and Preston, K. R. 1989. The baking performance of Canadian bread wheat classes using a Colombian high-fat high-sugar process. Can. Inst. Food Sci. Technol. J. 22:364-371.

Dexter, J. E., Kilborn, R. H. and Preston, K. R. 1990. The effect of formula variations and dough development method on Colombian aliñado bread properties. Cereal Chem. 67:46-52.

Faridi, H. and Faubion, J. M. 1995. "Wheat usage in North America" In: Wheat End Uses Around the World, eds. Faridi, H. and Faubion, J. M. , St. Paul, Minnesota: American Association of Cereal Chemists, pp 1-41.

Huang, SD and Miskelly, DM. 1991. "Steamed bread - a popular food in China," Food Australia, 43 (8): 346-47, 350-51.

Huang, S. and Ah, Q. 1994. "Steamed Bread Processing" in: Food Processing and Wheat Quality Improvement, ed., Z. Line, Beijing: Chinese Agricultural Publishing House, pp. 359-388 (in Chinese).

Huang, S., Quail, K. and Moss, R. 1995. Proceedings of the 45th Australian Cereal Chemistry Conference, September 10-14, 1995, Adelaide, p307-311.

Huang, S. and Quail, K. 1995. "Wheat Based Foods," Cereal International, autumn, p6-9.

Huang, S., Yen, S., Quail, K. and Moss, R. 1996. "Establishment of Flour Quality Guidelines for Northern Style Chinese Steamed Bread," J. Cereal Science 24 (2): 179-185.

Huang, S. and Quail, K. 1996. Proceedings of the 46th Australian Cereal Chemistry Conference, September 1-6, 1996, Sydney, p315-318.

Line, F. 1986. Florence Lin's Complete Book of Chinese Noodles, Dumplings and Breads. New York: William Morrow and Company, Inc.

McMaster, G. J. and Gould, J. T. 1995. "Wheat usage in Australia and New Zealand" In: Wheat End Uses Around the World, eds. Faridi, H. and Faubion, J., St. Paul, Minnesota: American Association of Cereal Chemists, pp 267-285.

Nagao, S. 1995. "Wheat Usage in East Asia" in: Wheat End Uses around the World, eds. Faridi, H. and Faubion, J., St. Paul, Minnesota: American Association of Cereal Chemists, pp167-189. 53(5): 1563-1565.

Peña, R. J. 1995. "Wheat usage in Mexico and Central America" In: Wheat End Uses Around the World, eds. Faridi, H. and Faubion, J., St. Paul, Minnesota: American Association of Cereal Chemists, pp 43-64.

Statistics Canada Report, 1996. Industry Profile- Canadian bread and bakery industry.

Yamada, Y. and Preston, K. R. 1992. Effects of individual oxidants on oven rise and bread properties of Canadian short process bread. J. Cereal Sci. 15:237-251.

Yamada, Y. and Preston, K. R. 1994. Sponge and dough bread: Effects of oxidants on bread and oven rise properties of a Canadian red spring wheat patent flour. Cereal Chem. 71:297-300

Zhu, J., Huang, S., O'Brien, L., Wei, X.. and Mares, D.J., 1997. Proceedings of the 47th Australian Cereal Chemistry Conference, September 14-19, 1997, Perth, p272-275.

The Compound Feed Industry and Food Animal Production

Kim B. Koch

Northern Crops Institute, North Dakota State University, Fargo, ND, USA

Introduction:

References regarding successful food animal production are found throughout recorded history and pre-date the appearance of commercial feed companies by many thousands of years. Thus, the following question needs to be asked.

"Why is there a livestock feed industry?"

I would like to suggest the following as answers.

1.) The feed industry provides a product and/or a service to terrestrial and aquatic food animal producers which they cannot provide for themselves, cannot provide at a competitive price, or cannot provide in sufficient quantity with required quality.

2.) The feed industry provides a market outlet for commodities, products and co-products deemed unsuited or inappropriate for human consumption. Animal feed is a value-added form of waste recycling.

As we look toward the future the next question seems obvious.

"Will the industry continue?"

I think the answer is, " Yes, some form of the feed industry will survive."

1.) Unless there is a major worldwide reordering of food preferences or resource availability, the demand for food animal products will continue.

(a) In many developed countries, demand for food animal products has reached maturity. Concerns about resource allocation, environmental impact and animal welfare may limit growth opportunities within the food animal production sector and the feed industry.

(b) Changes in consumer demand patterns for food animal products require adjustments in food animal production, resulting in redistribution of market share and reallocation of resources. Net result could be products from poultry and aquaculture supplanting significant portions of the market served by the beef, swine and dairy sectors.

2.) Historically consumers have demonstrated consistent increases in their demands for food animal products (meat, milk and eggs) as their buying (purchasing) power has increased.

(a) Asia and south east Asia have demonstrated the most potential for increased demand for food animal products and feed.

(b) This should stimulate expansion and growth in their feed industry and food animal production sector.

(c) Opportunities for importation of food animal products and necessary production inputs may develop in this region.

Background

Animal feed production began as an off-shoot of the commodity trading of cereal grains (maize, oats, barley, rye and wheat) and the flour milling industry. Its establishment was an effect of the industrialisation and urbanisation that occurred during the last quarter of the 19th century. Urban expansion pushed the support services (housing and pasture) needed for a horse powered economy farther and farther from the job site, just as it displaced fields and food animals. It became necessary to provide feed (forages supplemented with grains) for work horses housed in an urban setting. This practice of providing forage, grain and other inputs carried over to food animal production as well. The feed industry began with minimal capital investment and limited knowledge of animal nutrition. The Industry was restricted to locally available ingredients, and "state-of-the-art" processing technology was particle size reduction. Marketing and sales efforts were very limited and tended to be local in scope.

Throughout much of its history the feed industry changed very little in the way it formulated, manufactured and sold feed. It was a local business that used regional inputs and was not greatly concerned with nor impacted by global economic events. During the final decades of the 20th century, that has all changed.

The feed industry has evolved into a complex global enterprise that supplies and services producers of terrestrial and aquatic food animals. Global production of commercial compound feed in 1994 was 530 million metric tonnes (an additional 350 million metric tonnes was mixed on-farm and 220 million metric tonnes of single ingredients were used on-farm) (Wild, 1997). The industry responsible for that production has experienced wide-scale consolidation and downsizing. The survivors of this selective-reduction process have used aggressive proactive strategies to meet the demands of food animal producers and ultimately the consumers of food animal products. Where markets for food animal products have matured or are maturing, a renewed commitment to product and service development, marketing and sales is required. Market evolution in these countries has continued because food animal production increased even as the number of food animal producers declined and competition for market share increased. In market areas where increased demand for animal products is expected, feed companies are strengthening their positions and preparing for an expanded presence. Throughout the feed industry heightened awareness concerning the importance of food animal performance (cost of production) has stimulated research to identify ingredients, formulation techniques and manufacturing processes that offer increased or enhanced nutrient availability or improved nutrient utilisation. Ingredient supply and demand are viewed globally. Today's ingredient inventories are comprised of a bewildering array of raw and processed materials that are augmented by co-products and additives. Government involvement has ballooned to include regulation of additive use, label compliance, manufacturing standards and environmental correctness.

As the new millennium draws near, the feed industry and food animal producers are being challenged to find solutions to a number of complicated issues. These issues include resource availability and allocation, environmental impact, public concern of animal health and welfare, political issues (domestic and international) and global economic well-being.

Vision 2000

I believe there are three key areas which must be addressed to allow the full potential of the feed industry to be realised. First, compounded diets must be continually reviewed and upgraded so the production potential of food animals is optimised. The goal is to satisfy nutritional requirements during all stages of physiological development. Ingredient selection should be based on the following criteria: reliability of ingredient supply; consistent ingredient quality; and most importantly nutrient content, bioavailability and cost. Second, processing and manufacturing techniques that contribute to enhanced nutrient bioavailability and improved nutrient utilisation should be used whenever increased animal performance can be proven and economic cost justified. Some processes also offer improved hygiene and should be incorporated to provide increased food safety and strengthen consumer confidence in food animal products. Enzyme treatments that provide increased nutrient availability and utilisation should be explored. Third, leadership should enact and follow polices designed for long-term fiscal strength by encouraging responsible resource use. This means market segments should be thoroughly explored and marketing strategies developed based on the needs and expectations of the producers and consumers of food animal products.

The value-chain is being used more often when describing market structure and development. Grain growers, feed manufacturers, food animal producers and processors, and consumers of food animal products are all part of an extended value-chain. Each participant has a vested interest in the overall costs of producing and acquiring meat, milk and eggs. Since in a market economy the prices paid by consumers for food animal products are contingent upon the costs of feed manufacturing and food animal production/processing. The major costs associated with food animal production are feed, health maintenance of the animals, housing for the animals and labor. In feed production the major costs are ingredients, processing and manufacturing, labor, packaging and delivery, and marketing. Feed manufacturers and food animal producers/processors need profit margin (cost versus return) to be successful. Consumers of food animal products need food prices that take a minimal percentage of disposable income and allow increased return for food dollar spent. The efficiency with which the food animal converts inputs into products is the bottom line. If that conversion ratio does not allow for profit taking while at the same time satisfying consumer pressure for low cost food products, the chain breaks and all parties experience loss.

Numbers released by the USDA (Oct., 1997), Table 1, indicate expected food animal meat production (livestock and poultry) for 1998 in the U.S. to be 35.95 MMT. This is almost a 4% increase from 1997. The increased demand for maize to be used in feed for food animal production is projected in Table 2. Consumption of food animal meat (livestock and poultry) in the U.S. is reported in Table 3. The projected 1998 figure of 82.3 kg. is an increase of only 1%. There is general agreement that the upper limit of U.S. domestic consumption may have been reached. Support for increased domestic production will have to come from increased export activity. However, exports as a percent of total production may have peaked (Table 4). U.S. exports to Pacific countries are ranked in Table 5.

Table 1. U.S. Food Animal Production (livestock and poultry meat and eggs).

	1993	1994	1995	1996	1997*	1998*
	.... million tonnes					
Beef	0.428	11.240	11.415	11.554	11.500	11.284
Swine	7.740	8.026	8.950	8.095	7.743	8.409
Broiler	10.326	10.839	11.373	11.970	12.455	13.272
Turkey	2.203	2.269	2.331	2.484	2.484	2.602
Total	30.697	32.622	33.668	34.228	34.612	35.960
	.... million dozen					
Hen eggs	5,960	5,265	5,244	5,393	5,431	5,525

*Projections. Source: U.S. Department of Agriculture, October 1997

Table 2. U.S. Corn Supply and Use. _____

	million tonnes				
	1993-94	1994-95	1995-96	1996-97	1997-98*
Feed	115.461	135.859	115.633	132.496	139.909
Food/Inds. /Seed	38.978	41.555	38.855	40.745	42.790
Domestic Total	154.439	177.414	154.488	173.241	182.699
Exports	32.596	53.435	54.687	43.936	50.318
Total Use	187.035	230.849	209.175	217.177	233.017
Ending Stocks	20.863	38.241	10.456	21.698	17.574

*Projection. Source: Bob Wisner, Iowa State University, 1997

Table 3. Per Person Consumption (livestock and poultry meat).

	kg per person				
	1993	1994	1995	1996	1997*	1998*
Livestock	51.14	52.45	52.14	50.86	50.14	50.95
Poultry	28.45	28.27	28.86	29.23	31.05	31.32
Total	79.59	80.72	81.00	80.09	81.19	82.27
	number of eggs per person				
Eggs	239	236	234.6	237.2	239.7	243.4

*Projections. Source: U.S. Department of Agriculture, October 1997

Table 4. U.S. Broiler Exports as Percent of Total Production and Percent Increase.

	1993	1994	1995	1996	1997*	1998*
% production	9	12	16	17	17	16
% increase	32	46	36	14	5	3

*Projections. Source: Bill Helming and Joe Kropf, 1997

Table 5. 1996 U.S. Agriculture Exports: Leading Country Markets.

	Ag. Products	Position Bulk	Consumer Orientated
Japan	1	1	1
Republic of Korea	4	3	6
Taiwan	5	4	8
People's Republic of China	6	5	23
Hong Kong	8		4
Philippines	14	12	15
Indonesia	15	11	28
Malaysia	22	15	24
Thailand	23	20	33

Source: USDA, Foreign Agricultural Service, November, 1997

The International Food Policy Research Institute (IFPRI) presented the following statements and interpretations in two reports, "The World Food Situation: Recent Developments, Emerging Issues and Long-Term Prospects" and "International Model for Policy Analysis of Commodities and Trade"(Milling and Baking News, Nov. 4, 1997). Demand for cereal grains is expected to increase by 40% between 1993 and 2020, and demand for meat is expected to increase by 63% in the same time period. Developing counties will account for 80% of the increased cereal demand and 90% of the meat demand. Feed production will account for 24% of the cereals used in developing countries. The increased demand is stressing domestic marketing and processing systems. There is concern that in parts of Asia farm yields have reached economically optimum levels and inappropriate allocation of water along with declines in soil fertility will lead to limited yield improvement. Much of the increased demand will have to be satisfied through imports from developed countries. If Asian economies remain vital, this should not be a cause of worry. The U.S. could realise increased exports of 60% for cereal grains with Australia doubling its exports. Japan, South Korea, China and Taiwan are all major importers of cereal grains (Table 6). The economic well-being of these and other Pacific nations will determine just how much cereal grain they import for increased feed production.

Early forecasts by the U.S. Department of Agriculture projected global coarse grain use in 1998 at 890-895 MMT (USDA, July 1997). This projection included a 3.5% increase in consumption for Asia and Oceania. This area has seen increased demand for meat, especially poultry, and demand for coarse grains to be used in food animal diets has risen accordingly (Table 7) . However, year-end down trends in the economies of several Pacific countries undoubtedly will have a negative impact on these demand and use projections.

Table 6. U.S. and Australian Grain Exports 1995 - 1996.

	million tonnes		
	Barley	Maize	Sorghum
Australia	3.375		.594
U.S.	1.181	52.681	4.747

	Australia million tonnes		
	Barley	Maize	Sorghum
Destinations			
China	.912		
Japan	.550		.484
Taiwan	.132		

	U.S. million tonnes		
	Barley	Maize	Sorghum
Destinations			
Japan	.278	14.900	1.616
South Korea		7.333	
Taiwan		5.600	

Source: World Grain, November 1997

Table 7. Meat Production.

	Asia (million tonnes)		Oceania	
	1991 ... 1996		1991 ... 1996	
beef/veal	5.1	9.2	2.1	2.4
swine	29.4	47.0	.401	.425
poultry	10.1	19.9	.480	.603

Source: Food and Agriculture Organisation, 1997

Industry Trends

Consolidation

On a local and global scale, consolidation continues to be the major evolutionary force at work within the commercial compound feed industry. The top 10 U.S. feed companies from 1991 and 1996 are compared in Table 8. Particular interest should be given to those companies that maintained a presence on the list from 1991 to 1996.

Consolidation has allowed feed manufacturers to take greater control over input variables and provided an enlarged customer base (note the production figures). For some companies consolidation offered a way to remain active in the industry. Food animal production has become increasingly area and species specific, and consolidation has allowed feed companies to better serve their clients (note the changes in the percentages for pelleted and complete feed). As domestic and export markets for food animal products are found farther from the production site consolidation has helped supply the infrastructure needed to service them. Consolidation will continue as companies seek to gain and maintain competitive advantage by securing production resources and market share.

Table 8. Feed Company Profiles.

1991

Company	Mills	Production	Pellets	Complete
Purina Mills	62	4.545 MMT	60%	40%
Cargill (Nutrena Feed)	56	2.272 MMT	71%	55%
Central Soya (Master Mix)	26	1.181 MMT	75%	35%
Kent Feeds	23	1.363 MMT	45%	35%
Farmland Ind., Inc.	22	1.090 MMT	45%	30%
Agway	20	.968 MMT	80%	62%
Land O' Lakes	20	1.181 MMT	65%	30%
ADM (Supersweet Feed)	19	.682 MMT	65%	85%
Continental (Wayne Feed)	16	1.090 MMT	62%	35%
Southern States	10	.675 MMT	75%	80%

1996

Company	Mills	Production	Pellets	Complete
Purina Mills[1]	58	7.2 MMT	61%	65%
Cargill[2] (Nutrena Feed)	77	6.5 MMT	65%	50%
Gold Kist, Inc.[3]	16	4.0 MMT	90%	98%
Consolidated	52	3.0 MMT	70%	50%
Nutrition L.C.[4] PM Ag Products, Inc.[5]	40	3.0 MMT	8%	0%
Kent Feeds[6]	23	2.0 MMT	45%	5%
Farmland Inds., Inc.	24	1.82 MMT	58%	51%
Land O' Lakes	23	1.615 MMT	58%	69%
Continental (Wayne Feed)	16	1.5 MMT	30%	60%
Coast Grain Co.	3	1.3 MMT	6%	40%

Source: Feed Management December, 1991, Vol. 41, no. 12
Feed Management January, 1997, Vol. 48, no.1
1. includes Golden Sun Feeds
2. includes Walnut Grove, Farr Better, Young's and Wilco
3. includes Golden Poultry
4. includes Master Mix, Tindle, Lipscomb, Supersweet and Masterfeeds
5. includes Vigortone, Ag Products and Webel Feeds
6. includes Blue Seal Feeds and Evergreen Mills

Food Animal Health Maintenance

The U.S., along with other countries, is experiencing a trend toward industrialised production of specific food animals in concentrated areas. This has created many new challenges for both food animal producers and feed manufacturers. All parties in the food animal value-chain need to be concerned with animal health and well-being. Healthy, well cared for animals are more efficient users of inputs and therefore have a reduced cost of production, which makes them more cost efficient when compared with unhealthy, poorly cared for animals. Because of this cost saving advantage, both commercial and integrated feed manufacturers are being asked to take a more participatory role in food animal health management and maintenance. Any time large numbers of the same type of animal are reared in close proximity to one another, the risk of a catastrophic disease outbreak, parasite problem or natural disaster is magnified. If any of these scenarios came to pass the extended value-chain would be at risk because of the threat of disrupted production, which would call product consistency and uniformity, product quality and product safety into question. The feed industry and food animal producers are involved in large-scale pharmaceutical use to prevent and control disease and parasitic events. Used properly these products help keep production costs as low as possible, thereby keeping food costs down. Food animal producers should not be denied access to these very effective cost-lowering tools.

Concerns about possible overuse or misuse of antibiotics and the potential for loss of efficacy in humans due to evolution of resistant strains of bacteria has prompted both the Centers for Disease Control (CDC) and the World Health Organisation (WHO) to make strong statements opposing the use of sub-therapeutic levels of antibiotics for nutritional benefit or as "quick-fixes" for improper animal management (Feedstuffs, Oct. 27 and Nov. 10, 1997). It is imperative that a coalition of representatives from the feed industry and the food animal sector initiate proactive educational programs to inform consumers and the regulatory agencies charged with their protection about the importance of animal health products when related to food costs, food quality and food safety. Informed decisions must be made about what precautions are needed to safeguard the effectiveness of antibiotics while not sacrificing efficient production of food animal products.

In 1981 Swedish consumers and producers voiced strong concerns about the potential negative effects of unrestricted pharmaceutical use in food animal production. The Swedish government passed legislation in 1986 that required a veterinarian's prescription before antibiotics could be used in livestock feed. Professor J. Viaene (1997) reviewed the impact of this legislation on swine production and made the following points. The immediate result was a loss in productivity leading to increased costs of production. Evidence of this loss in productivity was threefold. First, increased incidence of diarrhoea in young animals was observed, which contributed to higher levels of weaning mortality. Second, daily gains in all stages of swine production decreased. Third, feed conversions were lowered. To combat these circumstances, veterinarians issued prescriptions for inclusion of therapeutic levels of antibiotics into all swine feeds. Total antimicrobial use has remained constant at about 35 MT per year, indicating that the legislation did not curb use.

Consumer concerns about food quality and safety should be respected. However, in a market that rewards low cost, domestic producers should not be put at a disadvantage because they are denied access to cost-lowering technology. This is especially true when consumers choose food animal products based on price.

Formulation

For years least-cost formulation has been used by feed manufacturers to meet minimum nutritional requirements at minimum cost. However, today they are being asked to provide food animal producers with feed products that are more than nutritionally adequate. The demand is for feed that is nutritionally optimal. Customised "best-use" feeding programs are being developed where the feed manufacturer works in partnership with the animal producer to challenge the food animals to their maximum genetic potential for conversion and gain. A "best-use" feeding program provides a win-win situation for the food animal producer. It offers increased performance levels with decreased production costs, and encourages responsible resource use with reduced environmental impact (lower manure generation).

The type of partnering used in "best-use" feeding programs began with the dairy sector. Feed company nutritionists worked with dairy producers to maximise milk yield by balancing available forages with proper concentrate use. Poultry integrators applied the concept to grains and protein sources and their success prompted the swine industry to adopt the practice. In all cases, the feeding programs are based on the genetic potential the food animals have for improved conversion of nutrients into lean tissue, milk or eggs. The potential of the animal is realised when the necessary nutrients are presented in the proper ratios at maximised availability. Thus, the quality of the ingredients used and the way they are processed is very important. Feed manufacturers are beginning to insist on very strict parameters with regard to the nutrient content of ingredients. Research has uncovered new synergistic and antagonistic relationships between ingredients and nutrient ratios. Advancements in process engineering have allowed feed manufacturers to provide improved nutrient availability in a wide range of ingredients.

Ingredients

Speaking before the North American Grain Export Association and the National Grain Trade Council, Harry D. Cleberg, president of Farmland Industries made the following statements. "Without a doubt, the grain of tomorrow will be customised, tailored to fit an individual buyer's needs;" "... industry must be transformed totally from its commodity orientation to one that builds trust among customers that the trade is willing to supply dependable, consistent and predictable products"(Milling and Baking News, Nov. 11, 1997). S.M. Shimoda of Bioscience Securities, Inc. (Feedstuffs, October 13, 1997) presented these comments to the National Agri-Marketing Association's, Issues Forum in Washington, D.C. "Biotechnology will redefine agriculture's value creation potential" and ".... this will turn many agricultural commodities into premium-priced specialty and quasi-specialty products."

Bulk generic commodity ingredients are being challenged by those claiming enhanced value. Enhanced value refers to the attributes of an ingredient that provide "value-in-use" to end-users. The attributes can be categorised as input, output and performance. For feed manufacturers and food animal producers "value-in-use" of a cereal grain is derived from all three. Input and performance attributes of enhanced grains provide incentive (improved pest and disease tolerance, increased yield) for producers to grow the crop. Output attributes offer improved nutrient content and bioavailability which can be translated into improved animal performance. The enhancement of the cereal grain provides "value-in-use" throughout the value-chain, with each transition of the chain receiving an equitable portion of the added or enhanced value.

Corn has been the leading feed grain for poultry and swine production in the U.S. for many years. Many poultry and swine diets contain at least 60% corn. Perhaps the best example of a specialty or enhanced value ingredient challenging an established commodity ingredient is high-oil corn (HOC). HOC is a recognised feed ingredient (Table 9).

Table 9. Partial Nutrient Composition of High Oil Corn (HOC) Varieties.

	Commodity			
	Corn	HOC[A]	HOC[B]	HOC[C]
moisture, %	14	14	14	14
crude fat, %	3.6	5.7	6.5	8.6
crude protein, %	7.9	8.3	8.4	8.9
poultry TME, kcal/kg	3390	3525	3560	3640
lysine, %	.25	.28	.29	.33
lysine, % of protein	3.16	3.37	3.45	3.71
methionine, %	.17	.19	.20	.21
TSAA, %	.37	.40	.40	.42
tryptophan, %	.057	.070	.070	.077

Source: Araba, 1997
A, B, C are different varieties of High Oil Corn

Araba, (1997) listed the following as potential benefits of HOC for feed manufacturers and food animal producers: reduced feed costs, reduced use and reliance on added fats and oils of poor or unknown quality, consistent source of metabolisable energy, uniformity in grain quality due to identity preservation throughout supply system and elimination of blending of inferior grades of corn. Production of HOC in the U.S. has grown steadily since its introduction. In 1996 there were 450,000 tonnes of HOC produced. That number increased by almost 56% in 1997 to 700,000 tonnes. Predicted production for 1998 is 1,800,000 tonnes, an increase of 57% (Feedstuffs, Oct. 27, 1997). In the middle of October 1997 it was announced that the Charoen Pokphand Corp., Ltd., of Taiwan had purchased 280,000 tonnes of HOC from Continental Grain Co. to be used in poultry diets. Charoen Pokphand controls about 35% of Taiwan's poultry market (Feedstuffs, Oct. 27, 1997).

Table 10. Barley and Naked Oats Fed in Combination to Growing-Finishing Swine.

	grain portion of diet					
% Corn	100					
% Barley		100	75	50	25	0
% Naked Oats		0	25	50	75	100
ADG, g	879	807	845	843	868	875
G/F		.38	.34	.35	.37	.39	.41
Dressing %	76.1	74.0	74.8	75.7	76.2	76.8
Shrink %	2.34	2.51	2.7	2.61	2.38	2.38
10th rib backfat, cm	2.5	2.18	2.2	2.14	2.55	2.5
LEA, cm sq.	40.3	42.2	43.2	45.3	43.4	40.3
Fat-free lean, g/day	328	317	321	345	333	333

Source: Harrold *et al.* 1997

Naked oats is another coarse grain which may become a value enhanced grain product used as a feed ingredient. There are indications that the output attributes of this grain provide improved nutrient availability when used individually. In addition, there appears to be a synergistic effect when naked oats are combined with barley. Indications are that such diets provide equal or improved performance when compared with standard corn-soy diets fed to growing/finishing swine (Table 10). Further modification of nutrient ratios will be required to fully understand the relationship between barley and naked oats. If input and performance attributes, can be made to match the output attributes, these grains may gain acceptance as replacements for corn. This could help reduce the demand on corn, which has been steadily increasing.

Process Engineering

Four basic types of processing are used in feed manufacturing. They are thermal and non-thermal, wet and dry, and they can be used separately or in combinations. The goal of processing is to provide increased nutrient availability or nutrient utilisation that is manifested by improved animal performance. A secondary benefit of thermal processing (wet or dry) is increased microbial destruction. Basic feed manufacturing can be accomplished using nonthermal dry processes. Included in these processes would be particle size reduction and mixing. Feed produced under these conditions can be improved by the introduction of a dry or wet thermal process. A wet thermal process would be steam flaking, pelleting or extrusion cooking, while micronising is a dry thermal process.

The pelleting process can be described as the agglomeration of a dry flowable mixed feed into compacted feed morsels. The transformation is accomplished by exposing the mixed feed to an application of steam (increased temperature and moisture) in a conditioner and then compressing it through a die hole. Improved performance of animals fed pelleted diets is well documented (Table 11). Behnke (1994) offered the following as reasons for the improved performance: decreased feed wastage, reduced selective feeding, decreased ingredient segregation, destruction of pathogenic organisms, thermal modification of starch and proteins, and improved palatability.

The pelleting process is a complicated series of relationships and compromises. Pellet quality has been related to pellet durability or resistance to breakage. It was generally believed that 60% of pellet quality was due to formulation and particle size. Feed manufacturers were forced to

Viaene, J., 1997, Antimicrobials Ban Hits Swedish Production, Feed Mix, vol. 5, no. 4, pp 27-29.

Wicker, D.B., 1995, The effects of Annular Gap Expansion on broiler feeds. Proc. 22nd Annual Carolina Poultry Nutrition Conf., pp 45-63, Charlotte, NC.

Wild, R., 1997, Snapshot of the World Feed Industry: Global Perspective. Feed Management, vol. 48, no. 7, pp 10-13.

Wondra, K.J., J.D. Hancock, K.C. Behnke, R.H. Hines and C.R. Stark, 1995, Effect of Particle size and pelleting on growth performance and nutrient digestibility, and stomach morphology in finishing pigs. J. Anim. Sci.,73:757.

Use of Cereals in Aquaculture Production Systems

H.Z. Saraç[1] and R.J. Henry[2]

[1]*Bribie Island Aquaculture Research Centre, Queensland Department of Primary Industries, Bribie Island , QLD, Australia*
[2]*Centre for Plant Conservation Genetics, Southern Cross University, Lismore, NSW, Australia*

Introduction

Aquaculture is becoming a major industry which produces a significant amount of the world's aquatic products. Today a wide variety of aquatic species, both animal and plant, such as fin-fish, crustaceans, molluscs, polychaetes, seaweed and algae is produced by farming across the world and production is rapidly increasing.

The World Aquaculture Industry consists of three major production systems. The most traditional system is the extensive production of aquatic plants and animals. This system mainly uses low stocking densities and the production relies mainly on the natural productivity of the environment. Farmers in this system contribute very little to the actual production. Although, in this system, only one species can be farmed, in most cases more than one aquatic species can be accommodated (polyculture) or one or more aquatic species could be farmed together with other terrestrial plants (rice) or animals (pigs or poultry) (integrated farming). This system is very common in south east Asia where aquaculture has been practiced traditionally for many centuries.

The semi-intensive aquaculture systems can also be carried out as a polyculture. The stocking density of the animals is higher than that in extensive systems. Farmers have to make some contribution to the natural productivity of the ponds by means of supplementing food. In this system, either pelleted complete aquatic feeds or trash feed such as minced offal, fish carcass and trash fish can be used depending on the availability and price of the feed.

The third system is called intensive aquaculture where stocking densities are high and the whole system depends on total support of the farmer. Ponds require regular water exchange and aeration, and animals are dependent on

Table 1. World aquaculture production and value (FAO, 1996).

	Production		Value	
	Tonnes	%	US$1000	%
Freshwater	12,456,218	67.1	18,699,317	55.8
Marine	6,098,897	32.9	14,831,496	44.2
Total	18,555,115	100	33,530,813	100

Table 2. Aquaculture production in 1994 by continents.

Continents	Production (%)	Value (%)
Asia	86.6	79.2
Europe	7.2	10.5
America (North)	3.1	4.2
America (South)	1.5	4.1
Former USSR area	0.8	0.9
Oceania	0.4	0.6
Africa	0.4	0.5
Total	100.0	100.0

Table 3. Production of farmed fin-fish in the Pacific-Rim Region.

Countries	Production (tonnes)		
	1992	1993	1994
China	5,387,10	6,526,63	7,966,47
Indonesia	406,07	460,15	490,11
Japan	353,14	343,62	346,99
Philippines	273,12	246,87	260,69
USA	258,95	278,44	252,12
Thailand	134,97	155,83	172,53
Vietnam	135,00	135,00	140,00
Chile	62,20	77,48	101,94
Russian Fed.	103,19	90,56	73,55
Canada	36,45	38,86	39,97
Other countries	132,05	134,54	143,57

formulated feeds. Artificial diets used in these systems are nutritionally balanced using various feed ingredients of both plant and animal origin. Depending on the species farmed the content and the source of carbohydrates in diets varies. For example, while barramundi (*Lates calcarifer*) can tolerate high levels of carbohydrates supplied with cereals, fish like salmon and trout need minimum carbohydrate content in their diets.

Aquaculture production in the Pacific Rim Region

The world aquaculture production is increasing at an average rate of 9.2% a year. Total production has exceeded 18.5 M tonnes with a total value of over US$33.5 billion in 1994 (FAO 1996). Therefore it is a very significant industry in the world. The majority of the production is in freshwater which comprises about 67.1% of the total production and 55.8% of the value (Table 1). Over the years the value of the farmed products has increased faster than the quantity of the produce (De Silva and Anderson 1995).

The major aquaculture industries could be divided into four basic groups; namely finfish, crustaceans, molluscs and aquatic plants. Increasing the amount of fin-fish and crustacean aquaculture requires a significant amount of feed substitution in various forms.

Asian countries produce 86.6% (79.2% in value) of the world production (Table 2). Europe and North America distantly follow Asian countries with 7.2% and 3.1% of world production, respectively. The Pacific Rim countries which include most of the major farmed seafood producing countries produce more than 90% of the world production.

The major fish and crustacean producing countries from the Pacific Rim area are China, Indonesia, Philippines, Thailand and the USA (Tables 3 and 4). Most species farmed in Asian countries are members of *Cyprinidae* family (carps) which have been traditionally farmed for over 2000 years (De Silva and Anderson 1995). Over 87% of the farmed fish in the Pacific Rim Region consists of non-carnivorous fish species such as carps, tilapia (*Oreochromis* sp), and milkfish (*Chanos* sp.) (Table 5) (FAO 1996).

Table 4. Production of farmed crustaceans in the Pacific-Rim Region.

Countries	Production (tonnes)		
	1992	1993	1994
Thailand	195,229	234,744	277,913
Indonesia	144,295	140,229	169,315
China	224,974	122,079	123,241
Exuador	113,987	86,272	99,531
Philippines	81,297	101,469	96,734
Vietnam	50,000	55,000	58,500
USA	30,738	28,916	24,422
Mexico	8,493	9,175	13,757
D.P. Rep.	13,000	13,000	13,300
Korea	9,486	7,337	8,954
Colombia	17,279	19,914	26,295
Other countries			

Most of these fish are produced in traditional extensive systems where very little or no artificial feed is used. However, the current trend is towards intensive farming in which more fish can be produced per unit of land. In addition many countries are replacing traditional farm species with high valued species such as reef fish species (coral trout) and Japanese king prawns in order to improve their economic return from aquaculture. These new trends require increasing inputs such as manufactured feeds which are formulated specifically for the requirements of the species farmed.

Aquaculture Feeds and cereals

Use of cereals in aquaculture varies greatly depending on the production system. Aquaculture practices are very complex in the Pacific Rim region since different countries mainly use traditionally driven methods to farm aquatic animals. In addition, there is a lack of information on the production of aquaculture feeds and amount of cereals used in these feeds in this region. Therefore, in this chapter we will use our estimations and the estimations made by other authors of feed production and the amount of cereals used in these feeds.

196

Table 5. Aquaculture production by species in the Pacific-Rim Region.

Species	Production (tonnes)		
	1992	1993	1994
Silver carp *Hypophthalmichthys molitrix*	1,576,274	1,842,069	2,160,284
Grass carp *Catenopharyngodon idellus*	1,236,338	1,469,296	1,793,935
Common carp *Cyprinus carpio*	601,218	1,109,278	1,352,620
Bighead carp *Aristichthys nobilis*	774,711	904,960	1,057,240
Nile tilapia *Oreochromis niloticus*	293,454	351,852	392,738
Crucian carp *Carassius carassius*	255,413	292,614	386,272
Milk fish *Chanos chanos*	318,150	313,414	334,156
White amur bream *Parabramis pekinensis*	181,516	218,921	281,625

New and Csavas (1993) have estimated that Asia produced a total of 1,558,721 tonnes of aquaculture feeds in 1990 of which 471,640 tonnes was for carnivorous fish feed, 554,206 tonnes was non-carnivorous fish feed and 532,875 tonnes was crustacean feed. They predicted that the total aquaculture feed production would be 2,662,854 tonnes by the year 2000. However, our estimations indicate that the total aquafeed production in 1994 was far greater (5,639,391 tonnes for the whole of the Pacific Rim region) than the estimation made for the year 2000 by New and Csavas (1993). The major reason for this is that aquaculture production has increased a lot faster than New and Csavas predicted. For example they predicted that the total aquaculture production in China would be 1,304,954 tonnes in 2000, but it had reached 7,966,000 tonnes in 1994. There are some differences in the countries included in our estimation and the estimation made by New and Csavas. However, these differences are not significant since Asian countries on the Pacific Rim region produce over 88% of the world's farmed fish and crustaceans.

Aquaculture production will increase as a result of increases in pond area, and intensification of extensive or semi-intensive production systems. Consequently, demand for aquaculture feeds will increase. With a 9% annual increase in aquaculture production, we estimate that 9.4 m tonnes of feed will be used in the Pacific Rim region in 2000.

Large quantities of cereals are produced in the world (Table 6). These cereals and by-products from their processing are relatively cheap ingredients for use in aquaculture feeds. Cereals such as barley are used predominantly as animal feeds (Sparrow *et al.* 1998) while species such as rice are largely consumed directly by humans. Cereals are important sources of ingredients for aquaculture feeds (Allan 1997).

Table 6. World Production of the Major Cereals (FAO 1991).

Species	Production 1990 (1,000 t)
Wheat	595,149
Rice	518,508
Maize	475,429
Barley	180,437
Sorghum	58,190

Use of cereals in aquaculture production systems

Cereal and fish polyculture

A significant amount of aquaculture farming in the Pacific-rim region is based on extensive fish farming in rice paddys. This is probably the oldest form of aquaculture, and today it is practiced in most Asian countries including China, Thailand, Taiwan, Vietnam, Laos and Indonesia. This is mainly based on growing carps, which graze on the ecology of the rice fields (Little and Edwards 1997). This is an integrated way of growing fish and rice in a environment symbiotic to both. Various organic components such as plankton, algae and plants grow in the rice paddys and provide nutrients for fish while fish droppings work as fertiliser for rice. Rice-fish culture is carried out using either tilapia, catfish, loach, gourami, snakehead, freshwater prawns or various carp species.

The cost factors involved in Aquaculture change dramatically depending on the country and the farming system. The major costs related to rice-fish farming are construction (35%), labour (34%) and seed fish (18%) in Indonesia (Koesoemadinata and Costa-Pierce 1992). On the other hand, in the Philippines labour is the only major cost item, constituting 50% of the total cost (Sevilleja 1992). However, the rate of return is always higher when rice is farmed together with fish. The rate of return from the rice-fish culture in Indonesia is around 68% to 107% of the total costs (Kangmin 1992). Sevilleja (1992) reports that the net return is 27% more in rice-fish farming in the Philippines, compared with rice monoculture. In Vietnam, the net return from rice-fish farming can be 176% higher than rice monoculture (Quyen *et al.* 1992).

In these systems, rice production can increase between 3% to 47% while farmers can harvest 232 to 1000 kg fish/ha (Kangmin 1992; Kim *et al.* 1992; Quyen *et al.* 1992; Sevilleja 1992). Higher fish yields occur when fish are given feed. It was estimated that if the rice-field culture has expanded to 6.6 million ha in three years, with the average rice production of 3 tonnes/ha, the national rice production in China could be increased by 2 m tonnes (Kangmin 1992). Rice-fish culture also helps eradication of weeds and harmful insects, loosening soils, increasing dissolved oxygen levels and improving the fertility of ricefields (Kangmin 1992).

Although rice-field farming has many advantages and a good future in Asia, there are some constraints which may hinder its development. The major constraint is the use of pesticides in rice-fish systems (Khoo and Tan 1980; Kangmin 1992; Koesoemadinata and Costa-Pierce 1992). Fish can act as a biological pest control in rice fields. However, some rice pests such as the yellow rice borer (*Tryporyza incertulas*) are very damaging and require the use of pesticides. In addition, other rice diseases such as sheath and culm blight (*Hypochnus sasakii*) and instant rice blight (*Xanthomonas oryzae*) have to be treated with pesticides. Most pesticides used in rice fields are toxic to fish. For example the LC_{50} of most pesticides is between 1 and 10 ppm in 48 hours for the common carp (*C. carpio*) (Kangmin 1992). Other factors which may affect the further development of rice-fish farming are the shortage of water and availability of fries of desirable species (Kangmin 1992; Koesoemadinata and Costa-Pierce 1992). Introduction of short duration rice varieties is also a limiting factor for the development of rice-fish culture (Kim *et al.* 1992).

Rice-fish farming is the best way of raising per unit yields in some Asian countries. However, it has to be recognised by governments as part of the larger agricultural system. Research must be carried out to develop ecological guidelines in order to identify the fish carrying capacity of rice fields. The effects of different quality and quantity of fertilisers, different cropping systems and soil type on the aquatic food web should be investigated (Koesoemadinata and Costa-Pierce 1992). Research must also be carried out on reduction of chemical use and the effect of chemical residues in fish on human consumption (Kim *et al.* 1992).

Cereals as supplementary feeds in aquaculture ponds

In semi-intensive aquaculture systems, cereals are used as fertiliser to increase the natural productivity of ponds and/or feed for fish (De Silva 1993). The main cereal and cereal products used as supplementary feeds are flour (wheat, barley, maize, rice, oat), whole grain (maize), bran (wheat, barley), hulls, bread crusts, noodle waste, and mill sweepings. Most cereal products are dispersed over the pond surface in powder form. The major advantage of using supplementary feeds such as cereals is to increase the fish yield by increasing the standing crop and the growth of the fish (Tacon 1990b). For example, it was reported that when Indian carp and Chinese carp were farmed together in India, the yield was 1053 kg/ha/year without fertiliser and supplementary feed. But the yield increased to 3314 - 4005 kg/ha/year when a supplementary feed mixture of rice or wheat bran and groundnut or mustard oilcake was used at 1:1 ratio (Sinha 1979). As a direct feed supplement, cereals are not very effective as a significant amount of feed is wasted. Fish are not able to ingest sufficient quantities of the feed supplement and are therefore not obtaining a nutritionally balanced diet. Nevertheless, uneaten feed supplement improves the natural food production in ponds thereby indirectly increasing fish yield (De Silva 1993).

The effectiveness of cereals as supplementary feeds depends on the physical form of the feed, the natural food supply in ponds and the standing crop of fish (Tacon 1990b; De Silva 1993). For example, 9% protein sorghum supplement did not affect carp production when the standing crop was 800 kg/ha (Hepher *et al.* 1971). In this situation natural food in the pond was enough to provide all nutritional requirements of the fish. However, when the standing crop was increased, the sorghum supplement had a significant effect on the fish production. Sorghum supplement was ineffective when the standing crop was further increased to 1,400 kg/ha. In this case, the natural food and sorghum supplement together were not enough to supply the nutrient demand of the fish. In semi-intensive culture systems, the quality and quantity of the natural food determine the rate of utilisation of the supplemented feed. From an economic point of view there are three options to obtain a balance between the natural food supply of the pond, standing crop and the utilisation of supplemented feed (De Silva 1993). The first option is to improve the diet by adding limiting nutrients. The second is to reduce the standing crop and the third is to increase the natural food in ponds by using fertilisers.

De Silva (1993) argues that supplementary feeds might be more favourable for farmers because of the high cost and poor availability of feed ingredients used in compound diets and increasing competition for these ingredients by users such as humans and stock animals. Therefore, more attention should be given to the effective use of the feed supplement in aquatic systems. It is recommended that future research in aquaculture feed developments should move away from traditional dose response studies on nutritional requirements of farmed species and on to the improvement of use of agricultural by-products (De Silva 1993).

Cereals as feed ingredients for aquatic animals

It is very difficult to estimate the amount of cereals used in aquaculture feed in the Pacific Rim region. However we speculate that the amount of cereals used in 1994 was between 1.0 m and 2.8 m tonnes. The majority of the cereals used were wheat and wheat by-products (germ meal, gluten, wheat middlings, bran, wheat shorts, wheat mill run and wheat pollards), rice and rice by-products (rice polishing and bran), maize and maize by-products (germ meal, gluten and bran), sorghum and dried brewers yeast.

Cereals are a very important part of aquaculture feeds and are mainly used as carbohydrate sources providing energy for the farmed aquatic animals. Starch especially from wheat is also used as a binder which works very efficiently when the feed is processed using steam. In addition to carbohydrates, cereals can provide proteins and lipids. However, special care should be taken in balancing the essential amino acid composition of aquatic feeds since cereal proteins are generally low in some essential amino acids such as lysine and methionine

Cereals can be used as ground whole seed as well as in the form of specific parts of the seed such as bran, gluten or hull. Gluten meals are the remaining section of the grains after the removal of the larger parts of starch and germ. Bran is the coarse outer covering of the grain kernel as separated from cleaned and scoured grain in the usual process of commercial milling. Hulls are the outer covering of the grain. There are other cereal products which are used as feed ingredients. For example, barley malt is the sprouted and heated whole barley grain from which the radicle has been removed. There is also middlings which is a by-product of flour milling that contains varying proportions of endosperm, bran and germ (Tacon 1990a).

Wheat

The nutritional composition of wheat varies greatly depending on the variety, soil fertility and the climate in which it is grown (McDonald *et al.* 1989). For example the protein content of wheat varies between 6 and 22% dry matter. The quantity and quality of protein and the quality of starch are very important when wheat is used in aquaculture feeds. Gluten which is the wheat protein present in the endosperm is an excellent binder since it posses the property of elasticity. A good quality wheat gluten should contain a minimum 60% protein (Akiyama *et al.* 1991). Although its high cost is a limiting factor for its use, wheat gluten is often used in extruded aquaculture feeds for species such as Japanese king prawns, barramundi and trout. For prawn diets, wheat flour should contain a minimum of 12% protein (Akiyama *et al.* 1991).Wheat gluten and wheat flour contents in aquaculture diets usually range from 0% to 10% and 20% to 35%, respectively.

Wheat by-products such as mill run, bran and middlings are often used in diets for semi-intensive systems. Some of these by-products are rich in protein and vitamins (New 1987). They also contain high amounts of fibre which is not suitable in formulated feeds especially those for prawns. High fibre levels in aquaculture feeds do not only dilute the nutrient content of the feed, but also reduce the stability of the feed pellets in water. Furthermore, fibre reduces the digestibility of feeds and creates water pollution.

Maize

This grain is often used in aquaculture feeds as a feed ingredient. It is an excellent source of energy, but is low in protein that is also poor in quality (McDonald *et al.* 1989). Maize is rich in vitamin A and contains about 70% starch. Maize is the source of two different types of protein, zein and gluten. Although zein is limiting in some essential amino acids such as tryptophan and lysine, maize gluten has reasonable levels of these amino acids. The protein content of the maize gluten is usually 20 - 30% (New 1987).

Rice

Rice is the main cereal crop in Asia and the most used cereal in aquaculture diets. Broken rice, which is the rice damaged during the dehulling and polishing of the rough rice, is a particularly common aquaculture feed ingredient in Asia. Rice has a thick fibrous husk similar to that of oats. The husk or hull can comprise up to 20% of the total weight of the grain (McDonald *et al.* 1989). Rice bran is rich in B group vitamins but high in fibre. Due to this fibre content, it should not be included in aquafeeds in large quantities. Similarly, inclusion of rice polishing should be limited since it also possesses a high fibre content.

Sorghum

This cereal is one of the main food grains in African and Asian countries. Although its kernel is smaller, it is very similar to that of maize. However, it has a higher protein and lower oil content. Use of sorghum in aquaculture feeds might be dependent on the tannin content of the grains. It is mainly used as ground whole grain.

Other cereals such as barley, oats, millet, triticale and rye can also be used in aquaculture diets. One of the issues in using cereals is their effect on the palatability of the diets. Increasing inclusion levels of cereals reduces the palatability of the aquaculture diets, especially for carnivorous species such as salmon, trout and marine prawns.

Composition of Cereals

Cereals contain large amounts of starch, cell wall polysaccharides and protein (Henry and Kettlewell 1996). These carbohydrates represent an energy source to those animals able to digest the polysaccharides and absorb the resulting sugars.

The endosperm cell walls in cereals are composed largely of arabinoxylans and glucans. The digestability of these polysaccharides, especially in aquatic animals is not well established.

Cereal proteins include groups of related storage proteins (Shewry 1996) some of which are deficient in amino acids essential for aquatic animal growth. The protein content and quality varies in different cereal tissues. The proteins of the embryo (germ) have a better amino acid balance than those of the starchy endosperm (storage proteins). Cereals are relatively poor sources of fats, however the germ contains higher levels than other grain fractions.

Nutritional value of cereals

Digestibility of cereals

Farmed fish and crustacean species can be grouped into four basic categories based on the nature of the food they ingest (De Silva and Anderson 1995).

1. Herbivores; (carp and tilapia) which mainly feed on plant materials.
2. Detritivores; (black tiger prawns) which largely feed on detritus.
3. Omnivores; (catfish) which mainly consume a mixture of food, both of plant and animal origin.
4. Carnivores; (trout and salmon) which only eat feed of animal origin.

All these animals are significantly different in terms of anatomy of their digestive tract. In general, they can be distinguished as fish with or without a stomach. Fish in the group without a stomach are those such as carp and with stomach are salmons, crustaceans, eels, tilapias, etc. Because of the differences in anatomy, nutritional behaviour and physiology, digestibility of feed ingredients differs significantly from species to species. Although, most fish species including crustaceans have major enzymes which are necessary for digestion, their activities are also effected by the species, feeding habits and living environment.

Carbohydrases are the most important enzymes for the digestion of cereals. They have a broad temperature tolerance (20^0C - 40^0C) and optimal activity usually occurs at pH 6 - 7 (De Silva and Anderson 1995). The activity of carbohydrases in fish depends on the feeding habit of the species (Table 7). For example, herbivorous fish such as carp have a higher activity of carbohydrases while activity is lower in salmon which are primarily carnivorous.

Digestibility coefficients of dry matter, protein and energy of some cereals for various fish and crustaceans are presented in Table 8. The differences in digestibilities are mainly due to quality of the ingredients, methodology used (inclusion rate of the ingredients, faecal collection period, type of marker used and analytical procedures), species and size of the animal, and the experimental conditions such as feeding rate. Digestibility of starches is generally good in herbivorous fishes. For example, common carp is able to digest 85% of the starch when its inclusion level is between 19% and 48% (Chiou and Ogino 1975). On the other hand a carnivorous fish species such as rainbow trout are able to digest only 24% to 52% of starches (Smith *et al.* 1980).

Table 7. Relative activities (max = 100) of amylase, α-glucosidase and ß- galactosidase in the digestive tract of various aquaculture species (De Silva and Anderson 1995).

Species	Amylase			α -Glucosidase			ß -Galactosidase		
	I	S	P	I	S	P	I	S	P
Carassius carassius (Crusian carp)	100						34		
Ctenopharyngodon idella (Grass carp)	84			100			61		
Oreochromis niloticus (Nile tilapia)	4	31					59		
Cyprinus carpio (Common carp)	35						8		
Hypophthalmichthys molitrix (Silver carp)	31						100		
Salmo gairdneri (Salmon)	8	<1	16				2	<1	
Anguilla japonica (Japanese eel)	1	<1		15	<1		20	11	
Seriola quinqueradiata (Yellowtail)	1	<1					22	6	

I, intestine; S, stomach; P, pyloric caecae

Table 8. Digestibility coefficients of energy, protein and dry matter of various cereals for various species of farmed fish and crustaceans.

Species	Cereals	Dry matter digestibility	Protein digestibility	Energy digestibility
Fish				
Chinook salmon	Extruded wheat[1]	75.75	87.4	67.5
	Wheat middlings[1]	31.4	85.7	45.3
Rainbow trout	Maize[2]	64.0	89.0	--
	Maize gluten[3]	--	79.8 - 86.8	70.9 - 87.3
	Maize gluten meal[4]	80.0	96.0	83.0
	Wheat[2]	68.0 - 72.0	90.0	--
	Wheat middlings[3]	--	65.3 - 67.7	39.6 - 52.8
	Wheat germ[3]	--	76.8	60.4
	Rice[2]	66.0	90.5	--
Channel catfish	Maize grain[5]	--	60.0	--
	Maize (cooked)[5]	--	66.0	--
	Wheat middlings[5]	--	72.0	--
	Wheat middlings[4]	35.0	92.0	46.0
	Wheat (extruded)[6]	--	92.0	--
Blue tilapia	Maize grain[7]	- -	84.0	--
	Maize (cooked)[7]	--	79.0	--
	Wheat[7]	--	90.0	--
Prawns				
Penaeus	Wheat gluten[8]	85.4	98.0	--
vannamei	Maize starch[8]	68.3	81.1	--
	Rice bran[8]	40.0	76.4	--
	Maize gluten[9]	--	92.9	--
Palaemon				
serratus	Maize[10]	--	87.6	79.1
	Wheat[10]	--	86.1	76.8
Macrobranchium	Wheat[11]	97.3	75.5	93.2
rosenbergii	Wheat[11]	86.1	74.6	79.1
	Barley[10]	--	88.9	78.4
	Rice bran[12]	88.6	91.8	--
Crayfish	Wheat bran[12]	78.7	95.7	--
Red swamp crayfish	Wheat gluten[12]	63.5	95.0	--

[1]Hajen *et al.* (1993); [2]Bergot (1993); [3]Smith *et al.* (1980); [4]Cho (1993); [5]Cruz (1975) [6]Wilson and Poe (1985); [7]Popma (1982); [8]Akiyama *et al.* (1991); [9]Foster and Gabbott (1971); [10]Ashmore *et al.* (1985); [11]Law *et al.* (1990); [12]Brown *et al.* (1986);

The digestibility of nutrients increases when the feeding level decreases in perch (Solomon and Brafield 1972) and channel catfish (Andrews 1979). Increasing the inclusion level of bread flour from 5% to 35% in diets for black tiger prawns improved the dry matter digestibility by 13% (Catacutan 1991). An increase in dry matter digestibility from 71.9% to 78.5% was obtained when the level of wheat starch was increased from 0% to 60% (Saraç *et al.* unpublished).

Digestibility increases when the cereals are processed prior to feeding. For example, extrusion improved the digestibility of energy in channel catfish (Wilson and Poe 1985). In black tiger prawns, pre-gelatinisation of wheat starch improved the digestibility of dry matter and energy (Saraç *et al.* unpublished). There is a positive correlation between the digestibility and gelatinisation of wheat starch in prawns (Figure 1). To improve the digestibility of cereals other processing methods such as sprouting and enzyme treatment could also be used (Marquardt 1993).

Nutrient utilisation

Previously, the nutritional importance of cereals appeared to be their capacity of binding other ingredients in formulated semi-intensive and intensive feeds. By doing that they keep most of the nutritional component intact in the feed until it is consumed by the target animal. Amongst the most recognised cereal binders are wheat flour (Pascual *et al.* 1978; Murai *et al.* 1981), glutinous rice flour (Murai *et al.* 1981), and maize starch (Pascual *et al.* 1978).

Cereals contain mainly carbohydrates and (Henry and Kettlewell 1996) therefore are mainly used in aquaculture diets as energy sources. Utilisation of carbohydrates by carnivorous fish species such as trout and salmon is limited. Increased levels of dietary available carbohydrate can cause depression in growth and some nutritional complications in carnivorous fish species (Reinitz 1980; Hilton and Slinger 1983). On the other hand some cereals improve growth when they are included in diets after treatments which improve their utilisation. For example, nutrient utilisation of maize is improved by extrusion and consequently food conversion ratio (FCR) is reduced in trout (Forneris et al. 1986). A positive effect of extrusion of carbohydrate sources such as maize and wheat on the availability of dietary energy was also demonstrated by Kaushik *et al.* (1989) in the rainbow trout (*Salmo gairdneri*). In contrast, omnivorous fish species such as tilapia and carp utilise carbohydrates better than carnivorous fish species. Tacon (1990a) reported that carp, channel catfish, tilapia and eels were more tolerant to the dietary carbohydrate levels than carnivorous fish species. These animals can effectively utilise carbohydrates as energy source and store any excess as body lipid.

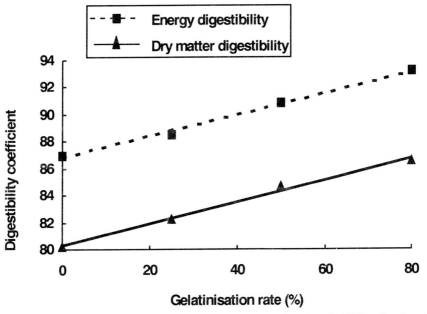

Figure 1. Relationships between the gelatinisation level (GL) of wheat starch and the digestibility coefficiency of dry matter (DM) and energy (E) in the black tiger prawns. DM digestibility = 0.0788GL + 86.834, R^2 = 0.99, P<0.5; E digestibility = 0.0813GL + 80.293, R^2 = 0.99, P<0.05.

The utilisation of carbohydrates varies depending on the complexity or chemical structure of the carbohydrate source used. Degani *et al.* (1986)

compared wheat meal, bread meal, soluble maize starch and sorghum meal in eels and found that wheat meal is utilised more efficiently than other cereals. Freshwater prawns (*Macrobranchium rosenbergii*) grew faster with diets containing barley as carbohydrate source than either maize, sorghum or wheat (Ashmore *et al.* 1986). Similarly it was reported that prawns (*Penaeus vannamei*) utilise wheat meal more efficiently than rice meal, maize, sorghum and millet (Cruz-Suarez *et al.* 1994). In terms of cost of production, prices of cheaper carbohydrate sources can overcome the effect of slightly lower growth rates and higher FCR's (Cruz-Suarez *et al.* 1994).

Fish and crustaceans can also utilise different cereals as protein sources at varying rates. However due to limiting levels of certain essential amino acids, cereal protein requires the addition of crystalline amino acids. Alternatively cereals should be used in conjunction with other protein sources which will compensate for the limiting essential amino acids. Ketola (1983) reported that diets with maize gluten as the sole protein source and some crystalline amino acid supplements improved the growth of rainbow trout. However, maize gluten by itself resulted in severe depression in growth, high mortality and erosion in caudal fins. However, Watanabe *et al.* (1993) reported that maize gluten can replace fish meal by up to 82% in diets for rainbow trout without any ill effects on growth rate, FCR and voluntary food intake.

Oils from cereals are used in diets for fish and crustaceans as either energy or essential fatty acid sources. Takeuchi *et al.* (1983) reported that the inclusion of maize oil in diets for tilapia resulted in better growth than pollack liver oil, beef tallow or medium chain triglyceride. Maize oil is also recommended for prawns (El-Dekour and George 1982) and trout (Arzel *et al.* 1994). Utilisation of maize oil by fish and crustaceans is associated with high concentration of polyunsaturated fatty acids in maize oil.

Cereals can influence the market value of the final product. For example ingestion of high levels of maize by carp may result in maize flavoured flesh (Mann 1983) which may not be desirable in some markets. Similarly, changes in flesh colour may also occur due to ingestion of cereals. Effect of changes in flesh colour on the value of fish can be very significant, especially when the product is a high value species such as salmon.

Conclusion

Cereals have an important role to play in aquaculture feeds. However, the more intensive forms of aquaculture allow only moderate levels of cereals in diets. Future research may result in the production of cereals better suited to aquaculture feeds. Genetic engineering of cereals (Henry and Ronalds 1994) may provide the tools necessary to achieve this objective. For example, specific grain components may be modified by modern molecular techniques (Henry 1997) so as to improve digestibility, availability or nutritional value.

References

Akiyama, D.M., Dominy, W.G. and Lawrence, A.L. (1991) Penaeid shrimp nutrition for the commercial feed industry: Revised. Proceedings of the Aquaculture Feed Processing and Nutrition Workshop. 19 - 25 September 1991. American Soybean Association, Singapore, pp. 79-98.

Allan, G.L. (1997) Alternative feed ingredients for intensive aquaculture. Recent Advances in Animal Nutrition in Australia, University of New England, Armidale.

Andrews, A.J. (1979) Some effects of feeding rate on growth, feed conversion and nutrient absorption of channel catfish. Aquaculture, 16:243-246.

Arzel, J., Martinez-Lopez, F.X., Metailler, R., Stephan, G., Viau, M. and Gandemer, G. (1994) Effect of dietary lipid on growth performance and body composition of brown trout (*Salmo trutta*). Aquaculture, 123:361-375.

Ashmore, S.B., Stanley, R.W., Moore, L.B. and Malecha, S.R. (1986) Effect on growth and apparent digestibility of diets varying in grain source and protein level in *Macrobranchium rosenbergii*. J. World Maricult. Soc., 16:205-216.

Bergot, F. (1993) Digestibility of native starches of various botanical origins by rainbow trout (*Oncorhynchus mykiss*). In ' Fish Nutrition in Practice',

S.J. Kaushik and P. Liquet (eds), pp. 857-866.

Brown, P.B., Williams, C.D., Robinson, E.H., Akiyama, D.M. and Lawrence, A.L. (1986) Evaluation of methods for determining in vivo digestion coefficients for adult red swamp crayfish *Procambarus clarkii*. J. World Aquculture Soc., 17:19-24.

Catacutan, M.R. (1991) Apparent digestibility of diets with various carbohydrate levels and the growth response of *Penaeus monodon*. Aquaculture, 95:89-96.

Chiou, J.Y. and Ogino, C. (1975) Digestibility of starch in carp. Bull. Jap. Soc. Sci. Fish., 41:465-466.

Cho, C.Y. (1993) Digestibility of feedstuffs as a major factor in aquaculture waste management. In 'Fish Nutrition in Practice', S.J. Kaushik and P. Liquet (eds), pp. 365-376.

Cruz, E.M. (1975) Determination of nutrient digestibility in various feedstuffs for channel catfish. PhD. dissertation, Auburn University, Alabama, U.S.A.

Cruz-Suarez, L.E., Ricque-Marie, D., Pinal-Mansilla, J.D. and Wesche-Ebelling, P. (1994) Effect of different carbohydrate sources on the growth of *Penaeus vannamei*: Economical impact. Aquaculture, 123:349-360.

Degani, G.; Viola, S. and Levanon, D. (1986) Effects of dietary carbohydrate source on growth and body composition of the European eel (*Anguilla anguilla* L.). Aquaculture, 52:97-104.

De Silva, S.S. (1993) Supplementary feeding in semi-intensive aquaculture systems. Proceedings of the Regional Expert Consultation on Farm-Made Aquafeeds, 14-18 December, 1992, Bangkok, Thailand, pp. 24-60.

De Silva, S.S. and Anderson, T.A. (1995) Fish Nutrition in Aquaculture, Chapman & Hall, London.

El-Dekour, S. and George, K.A. (1982) The effects of different dietary lipids on the growth and survival of *Penaeus semiculcatus*. Annu. Res. Rep. Kuwait Inst. Sci. Res., 1981:93-96

FAO, (1991) Production Year Book 1990. Vol. 44 FAO, Rome

FAO, (1996) Aquaculture Production Statistics, Fisheries Information, Data and Statistics Unit, FAO Fisheries Department, FIDI/C815(Rev. 8), FAO, Rome

Forneris, G., Boccignone, M. and Damasio, L. (1986) Extruded maize in rainbow trout (*Salmo gairdneri*) feeding. Riv. Ital. Piscic. Ittiopatol., 21:59-62.

Forster, J.R.M. and Gabbott, P.A. (1971) The assimilation of nutrients from compound diets by the prawns *Palaemon serratus* and *Pandalus platyceros*. J. Mar. Biol. Ass. U.K., 51:943-961.

Hajen, W.E., Higgs, D.A., Beames, R.M. and Dosanjh, B.S. (1993) Digestibility of various feedstuffs by post-juvenile chinook salmon (*Oncorhynchus tshawytscha*) in sea water. 2. Measurement of digestibility. Aquaculture, 112:333-348.

Henry, R.J. (1997) Practical Applications of Plant Molecular Biology, Chapman & Hall, London.

Henry, R. J. and Kettlewell, P.S. (1996) Cereal Grain Quality, Chapman & Hall, London.

Henry, R.J. and Ronalds, J. A. (1994) Improvement of Cereal Quality by Genetic Engineering, Plenum, New York.

Hepher, B., Chervinski, J. and Tugari, H. (1971) Studies on carp nutrition III. Experiments on the effects of fish yields of dietary protein source and concentration. Bamidgeh, 23:11-37.

Hilton, J.W. and Slinger, S.J. (1983) Effect of wheat bran replacement of wheat middlings in extrusion processed (floating) diets on the growth of juvenile rainbow (*Salmo gairdneri*). Aquaculture, 35:201-210.

Kangmin, L. (1992) Rice-fish farming systems in China: Past, present and future. Rice-Fish Research and Development in Asia. ICLARM, pp. 17-26.

Kaushik, S.J., Medale, F., Fauconneau, B. and Blanc, D. (1989) Effect of digestible carbohydrates on protein/energy utilisation and on glucose metabolism in rainbow trout (*Salmo gairdneri* R.). Aquaculture, 79:63-74.

Ketola, H.G. (1983) Requirement for dietary lysine and arginine by fry of rainbow trout. J. Anim. Sci., 56:101-107.

Khoo, H. and Tan, E.S.P. (1980) Review of rice-fish culture in Southeast Asia. In 'Integrated Agriculture-Aquaculture Farming Systems', R.S.V. Pullin and Z. Shehadeh (eds.). ICLARM, pp. 1-14.

Kim, B.H., Kim, H.D. and Kim, Y.H. (1992) Rice-fish farming systems and future prospects in Korea. Rice-Fish Research and Development in Asia. ICLARM, pp. 63-67.

Koesoemadinata, S. and Costa-Pierce, B.A. (1992) Development of Rice-Fish Farming in Indonesia: Past, present and future. Rice-Fish Research Development in Asia. ICLARM, pp. 45-62.

Law, A.T., Chin, K.S.S., Ang, K.J. and Makarudin, M.S. (1990). Digestibility of low cost ingredients in pelleted feeds by Macrobranchium rosenbergii (De Man). The Second Asian Fisheries Forum, Asian Fisheries Society, Manila, Philippines, pp. 333-336.

Little, D.C. and Edwards, P. (1997) Contrasting strategies for inland fish and livestock production in Asia. Recent Advances in Animal Nutrition in Australia'97. pp. 75-87.

Mann, H. (1983) The influence of nutrition on odour and flavour of fish. Optimierung von Betriebsparametern in der Aquakultur, 39:102-110.

Marquardt, R.R. (1993) Enhancement of the nutritive value of cereals (wheat, oats, barley and rye) and lupins for poultry by the inclusion of enzymes in the diet. Proceedings of the Ninth Australian Poultry and Feed Convention, 10- 13 October 1993, Gold Coast, Australia, pp. 74- 79.

Mcdonald, P., Edwards, R.A. and Greenhalgh, J.F.D. (1989) Animal nutrition. Longman Scientific & Technical, New York.

Murai, T.; Sumalangkay, A. and Pascual, F.B. (1981) The water stability of shrimp diets with various polysaccharides as a binding agent. Q. Res. Rep. SEAFDEC, 5:18-20.

New, M.B. (1987) Feed and feeding of fish and shrimp. FAO, Aquaculture Development and Coordination Programme, ADCP/REP/87/26, FAO, Rome.

New, M.B. and Csavas, I. (1993) Aquafeeds in Asia - A Regional Overview. Proceeding of the Regional Experts Consultation on Farm-Nade Aquafeeds, 14-18 December 1992, Bangkok, Thailand, pp. 1-23.

Pascual, F.P., Bandonil, L. and Destajo, W.H. (1978) The effect of different binders on the water stability of feeds for prawn. Q. Res. Rep., SEAFDEC, 2:31-35.

Popma, T.J. (1982) Digestibility of selected feedstuffs and naturally occurring algae by tilapia. PhD. dissertation, Auburn University, Alabama, U.S.A.

Quyen, M.V., Duong, L.T., Son, D.M., Minh, P.N. and Nghia, N.D. (1992) Ricefield aquaculture systems in the Mekong delta, Vietnam: Potential and reality. Rice-Fish Research Development in Asia, ICLARM, pp. 105-115.

Reinitz, G. (1980) Growth and survival of lake trout fed experimental starter diets. Prog. Fish-Cult., 42:100-102.

Saraç, H.Z., Kelly, B.J., Thaggard, H.B., Nash, M., Gravel, M.R. and Rose, J. (unpublished) Digestibility of starches by the black tiger prawn (*Penaeus monodon*).

Sevilleja, R.C. (1992) Rice-fish farming development in the Philippines: Past, present and future. Rice-Fish Research Development in Asia. ICLARM, pp. 77-89.

Shewry, P.R. (1996) Cereal grain proteins in Cereal Grain Quality, Henry R.J. & Kettewell, P.S., Eds. Chapman & hall, London, pp. 227-250.

Sinha, V.R.P. (1979) Contribution of supplementary feed in increasing fish production through composite fish culture in India. Proceedings of the World Symposium on Finfish Nutrition and Fish Feed Technology, Hamburg, 20 - 23 June, 1978. Vol. 1, Berlin, pp. 565-574.

Smith, R.R., Peterson, M.C. and Allred, A.C. (1980) The effect of leaching on apparent digestion coefficients in determining digestible and metabolisable energy of feedstuffs for salmonids. Prog. Fish. Cult., 42:195-199.

Solomon, D.J. and Brafield, A.G. (1972). The energetics of feeding, metabolism and growth of perch (*Perca fluviatilis* L.). J. Anim. Ecol., 41:699-718.

Sparrow, DHB, Lance, R.C.M. and Henry, R.J. (1988) Alternative End Uses for Barley. Royal Australian Chemical Institute, Melbourne.

Tacon, A.G.J. (1990a) Standard Methods for the Nutrition and Feeding of Farmed Fish and Shrimp - Nutrient Sources and Composition. Volume 2. Argent Laboratories, Washington, 129 pages.

Tacon, A.G.J. (1990b) Standard Methods for the Nutrition and Feding of Farmed Fish and Shrimp - Feeding Methods. Volume 3. Argent Laboratories, Washington, 208 pages.

Takeuchi, T., Staoh, T. and Watanebe, T. (1983) Dietary lipids suitable for the practical feed of *Tilapia nilotica*. Bull. Jap. Soc. Sci. Fish., 49:1361-1365.

Watanabe, T., Pongmaneerat, J., Sato, S. and Takeuchi, T. (1993) Replacement of fish meal by alternative protein sources in rainbow trout diets. Nippon Suisan Gakkaishi, 59:1573-1579.

Wilson, R.P. and Poe, W.E. (1985) Apparent digestibility of protein and energy in feed ingredients for channel catfish. Prog. Fish-Cult., 45:154-158.

Uruguay 4-5
USA 13-15, 23, 26, 91, 101,
   140-142, 171, 195
USDA 175, 177-178, 189-190

----- V -----
vacuum 40, 43, 45-46, 49, 56,
   61, 63-65, 74, 84, 87, 89,
   130, 153
varieties 4, 14, 97, 107-109,
   112, 116-119, 127, 161,
   164, 168, 184, 188, 200
variety 3, 13, 16-17, 19, 33,
   93, 97, 107, 116, 123,
   126-127, 130, 150, 153,
   157, 163-164, 166, 193, 202
Vermicelli 20
Vietnam 26, 36, 199, 215
vinegar 25, 152
ViscoAmylograph 96
viscograph 133
viscosity 33, 96, 109, 133,
   136-137
vitamins 160, 203

----- W -----
Wafers 22
Waffle 22
warm 29, 162
wasabi 25
waxy 32, 93-94, 96
Wheat 1, 3, 5-11, 13-19,
   21-23, 25, 37, 67, 88, 91,
   93-94, 96-97, 99-101,
   104-105, 107-110, 112,
   116-119, 123, 125-130,
   132-135, 138, 141-148, 150,
   153-154, 157, 166, 168-170,
   172, 187, 198, 200,
   202-203, 208-210, 213-215
wheaten 123, 143, 168
whiter 135
wrapped 26, 36, 153
wrinkles 82

----- X -----
xanthan 137
xanthophylls 130-131

----- Y -----
Yeast 22, 145-146, 148-149,
   152, 160, 165, 202
Yellow 16, 101, 108, 116,
   123, 130-131, 136, 138,
   159, 200
yellowness 106-108, 117, 138

----- Z -----
zein 203

225